AUTUMN LADY is the third book Mama San
has written about her life with one of the greatest
teachers of our time: T. Lobsang Rampa.

In her reminiscences of their fascinating life
together, she shows the followers of the great man
the human side of this amazing being. She also
brings to life more of the intriguing cat-people
who watch over them both.

Also by Mama San Ra'Ab Rampa

PUSSYWILLOW
TIGERLILY

and published by Corgi Books

Mama San Ra'Ab Rampa

Autumn Lady

CORGI BOOKS
A DIVISION OF TRANSWORLD PUBLISHERS LTD

AUTUMN LADY
A CORGI BOOK 0 552 11283 6

First publication in Great Britain

PRINTING HISTORY
Corgi edition published 1980
© Mama San Ra'Ab Rampa 1980

Corgi Books are published by Transworld Publishers Ltd.,
Century House, 61-63 Uxbridge Road,
Ealing, London, W.5.
Made and printed in Great Britain by
William Collins Sons & Co Ltd, Glasgow

Every new dawn brings a fresh promise.

President Sadat of Egypt

The Woman asked, *'What of Children?'* and he answered:

'You may give them your love but not your thoughts,
For they have their own thoughts.
You may house their bodies but not their souls,
For their souls dwell in the house of Tomorrow
Which you cannot visit, not even in your dreams.
You may strive to be like them,
But seek not to make them like you
For life goes not backward, nor tarries with Yesterday.'

Gibran.

CONTENTS

'Ignorant people think it's the noise which
fighting cats make that is aggravating, but
it ain't so; it's the sickening grammar
they use.'

Mark Twain

ONE

'She was an autumnal lady therefore it was fitting she should
depart in the autumn.' One of Miss Taddy's friends made
the above comment, and it seems a fitting tribute to our
Tadikins who had always appeared older than her years,
she who in her own special way had brightened our lives,
especially mine, during the whole span of her life. She
earned the name 'Tad' because, as a kitten, she was so tiny,
much smaller than her sister, who enjoyed the royal name
of Cleopatra. Later it was decided little Tad should receive
a name of equal importance – so for important occasions
she became Miss Tadalinka Rampa; at home she was Taddy
or Tadikins.

Of course cats are acknowledged to be the possessors of
at least three names – one by which they are known to the
Family, the human Family, and to which they will sometimes answer, when called, and a second which is decided
upon by the cat person and his cat acquaintances. For the
third title one cannot do better than turn to the poet T. S.
Eliot on *'The Naming of Cats'* – where he says – and I
quote a few lines:

'But above and beyond there's still one name left over,
And that is the name that you never will guess:
The name that no human research can discover –
But THE CAT HIMSELF KNOWS, and will never
     confess.'

Although our Taddy often gave one the impression of
being lethargic, and interested mainly in food, it is my belief that she was a very alert Cat Person, and I have it on
good authority, as well as from my own observations, that
she was extremely telepathic, extremely psychic. Often we
called her 'the telephone girl' because she was so mentally
alert even when apparently lacking in physical energy. How
often I have mulled over the reason for this creature's
determination to become a member of my Family, for determined she was, as various episodes proved. Of course it
was worth more than a little effort to get oneself accepted
into a Family where Lobsang Rampa was the chief member, and after two or three tries the goal was achieved. But,
as with everything worthwhile, it took time.
    Everything in life takes time, nothing 'comes easy' and
now we have to go back about a decade and a half where
the thread of our tapestry has its beginnings. We had been
living in Canada for only a very few years, arriving first to
Windsor, Ontario, accompanied by two feline ladies well
known to readers of the Rampa books, Mrs Fifi Greywhiskers and Miss Ku'ei. Our stay in that city has been
fairly well documented in my first book, *Pussywillow*, so
repetition is unnecessary. One of our Windsor acquaintances expressed astonishment when we happened to mention we seriously considered moving to the, then small,
town of Fort Erie, on the Niagara river. This man remarked,
'You won't like it there – it is only suitable for tourists.'
However, fate, or whoever decides these things decreed that

Fort Erie was to be our destination and that is where we found ourselves, on the edge of the Niagara river.

After living for about a year at Cedar House we decided to move into the town, into a small apartment building, at what is known as the South End, and quite near Peace Bridge which spans the river between Fort Erie and Buffalo, New York State. Since this building had quite obviously seen better days, the accommodation was far from comfortable, and once there was an invasion of ants. When we spread anti-ant spray on the floor Miss Ku'ei became sick after stepping on it, and washing it from her paws. She was not a very placid patient at any time, so that was another problem.

Well, eventually we heard of a little house for rent, just one street beyond Jarvis, which was the centre of town, where most of the very few stores were located, also the Main Post Office. To be living at ground level seemed quite strange after being 'in the air' but soon we were adjusted, and we had the added pleasure of a small garden, a delight to the Siamese people. On looking back I do not think Fort Erie was anything like ideal for such a family as ours, it was too small and, apart from a few outstanding personalities, most people's outlook was too narrow.

Just as we felt we had reached another dead-end and were considering our next step, an outside influence invaded us in the form of a letter, leaving us with another problem to solve; another decision to make.

One morning, as the Guv began sorting his mail, he came across one missive which instantly attracted his attention. (I should mention that the Guv is the name by which Lobsang Rampa is known to the Cat People – as readers of my previous books will know, so it seems convenient to continue its use.) Well, the Guv held the letter for a second while we all became silent, even the Cat People, and then

11

he opened the envelope. After reading the letter twice he looked up. 'There's something still in the envelope,' I said. The Guv examined the envelope again and pulled out a photograph which showed a very busy man, a man sitting at a large desk with a telephone in front of him. At his side was a large tape-recording machine, together with an equally large IBM electric typewriter.

All this appeared most impressive and by this time I was eager to know the reason for the letter which bore an impression of authority. The Guv asked me what I thought about taking a trip to South America, and he passed the letter to me for my comments. It was, in short, an invitation to visit that small country, Uruguay, which is bordered by another small country, Paraguay, and by that large landmass, Brazil.

Apparently Lobsang Rampa was a very popular author in South America and we were advised that it would be good publicity to appear in Argentina, that large Spanish speaking country, as well as in Uruguay. Our tickets would be bought by a group of interested persons known as *los amigos de Lobsang Rampa* – the friends of Lobsang Rampa, and a second letter arrived while we were still contemplating the first. This time we were urged to lose no time in making preparations for the journey, that every facility was at our disposal including typists, interpreters, and that a large office was available for our use. The 'friends of Lobsang Rampa' apparently were most enthusiastic.

Mr U, as I will call him, showed great interest in Mrs Fifi Greywhiskers, and he wanted to use all his resources in the promotion of her book, *Living with the Lama*. When eventually we did reach Montevideo, without Fifi, the gentleman was most displeased and he made quite a display of anger, acting as though we were to blame for the situation.

12

Do not follow where the Path may lead.
Go, instead, where there is no path
and leave a trail.

TWO

Before reaching a final decision the matter was given much thought – we are not the type to go careering around the world for no useful purpose and, although Lady Ku'ei Cat loved travelling, we were not anxious to submit Fifi Grey-whiskers to unnecessary hardship. She was satisfied doing whatever the Family considered best but, given the choice, would have preferred no more jaunts.

However, as these people appeared so anxious to receive us into their midst, and we had no other plans, it seemed best that we make the effort, hoping the result would make the venture worthwhile.

It would be a further six months before we were to depart, and it seemed a very long wait, while letters would be exchanged between Lobsang Rampa and Mr U on behalf of the *amigos*.

It was a beautiful summer and we spent it mainly in our little garden, where Fifi and Ku'ei loved to play around the flowers and trees, while we were just 'ticking over' and waiting. Once while I was alone with the Cat People I saw another feline in the vacant lot adjoining ours, and he seemed to be playing with something which I judged to be a bird. When I went over to the cat he ran away and I rescued the little bird, who was suffering more from fright than anything, and after he recovered he flew off. A few days later I witnessed the same scene again, but in our garden, and this time I was not so lucky for the cat had won. Possibly, if it was the same little sparrow, it may have become too trusting after being kindly treated by a human, not realizing the necessity of remaining constantly alert.

There were various documents to be prepared, and we had to go along to another district, Ridgeway, where we visited a most agreeable medico who gave us 'shots' before the documents could be completed. Fifi and Ku'ei would not have their papers until later for their inoculations would be valid for a much shorter period, therefore they had to be delayed until just before leaving.

Not only was it a lovely summer that year but the warm weather continued late into autumn, right to November, something quite unusual for, in that part of the world, one had to be prepared for cold, unpleasant days by October at the latest.

Fifi loved the warm sun and in the early afternoon she could be found just inside the side door of our house, where the upper part was of glass. For thirty minutes or so she would sit there contentedly washing until old Sol moved along, when she would return to her place with the Family.

During those days of waiting we enjoyed an occasional visit from a lady we had come to know while at Cedar House, her home being a short distance from us, on the Parkway where she lived with her husband. Gladys, like ourselves, loved birds and all animals, and cared for them during the hard winter months; all kinds of feathered creatures would assemble in the garden chirruping for attention.

Gladys had COLOUR, always her conversation was full of interest, and she was very artistic, her interest being oil painting. Another hobby was copper-enamelling, and the extent of her imagination was evident in the designs she

14

executed. Once she arranged a display at a store in Niagara Falls, and we were pleased to know of its success, and to hear how many items had been sold. Apart from her skills she was, and is, a most attractive person, physically as well as intellectually.

So the days wore on towards the time of departure and a truck collected our big pieces of luggage, after which they would be sent on to New York, ahead of us. Still we had to wait a little longer and any moment our tickets would be arriving. At last it was time to make final arrangements with the bank, and the post office, for even in those far off days Lobsang Rampa was getting a considerable volume of mail. Pauline, whom we had come to know quite well, agreed to forward our letters, a service for which we were most appreciative, and which she carried out for a number of years, long after we returned to Canada – until about two or three years ago when we cancelled the Fort Erie postal box. Pauline, like us, had come to this country from England, and we will always have a kind feeling towards her for her efficient and willing service.

At the last moment, after our departure, Gladys would deal with the closing of our little house and hand in the keys to the landlord and this little duty she was happy to perform. She came to bid us goodbye on the last evening, and it is the same how ever many times we go on a journey, and wherever we go; it is always a time of apprehension, tinged with sadness, not knowing how long we will be gone, whether we will all meet again and where.

We were to travel from New York by freighter, on the Moore McCormack line, the particular vessel was the *Mormactrade*. There is no ship's doctor on a freighter so the maximum number of passengers they are allowed to carry is twelve persons. Not many people were travelling to South America at that time because it was the period of the Cuban Missile Crisis, and everybody was waiting for the outcome between the US and Russia. Within a year, on the assassination of the President, America had further cause for concern.

If you can't dream what have
you got to come true!

Elvis Presley.

THREE

At last the moment of departure was upon us, and we gathered our things together while our thoughts were of the immediate future, wondering whether we were taking the right step, knowing there is no standing still if one wants to progress.

It is best to start a journey early in the day but for us there was no choice except to go in the evening, since that was the time to catch the train to New York. Fifi had settled herself down for the night so it saddened me to disturb her; she had lived a long time and at this stage she needed to take life quietly.

A knock on the door and the driver announced himself, so we took our places in the station wagon, complete with our hand luggage, leaving Fort Erie behind, and speeding across Peace Bridge to the Buffalo railway station, from where we would travel overnight, reaching New York in the morning.

Of course we had sleeping berths but one cannot sleep well on a train, not me anyway, and Miss Ku'ei kept calling to tell me each time we passed a station. She always seemed to come to life when there was any activity – while Fifi was exactly the opposite. Fifi stayed close beside me all the way, secure in the knowledge that her days of misery, of being stuffed in a suitcase while being banged around, were over.

17

In the early hours of the morning we reached New York Central station and as the train pulled in to the platform there seemed to be a tremendous bustle of activity. So we alighted, feeling somewhat lost, but soon a porter, a Red Cap, came along, grabbing our suitcases and slinging them on to a trolley. We had to prevent him from taking Fifi and Ku'ei, in their carrying baskets and piling them on top too; we preferred to transport them ourselves because they too were 'People'.

Soon we were safely ensconced in the station hotel, the Commodore, where we would stay for a few hours, until the afternoon, when we would make our way to the dock area, there to be met by the *Mormactrade* personnel, and shown to our suite. For those who do not care for social life a freighter offers the best opportunity of enjoying sea travel, much to be preferred over a purely passenger ship. The nearest approach to being sociable on a freighter is to be pleasant to the ship's captain and, if he approves, you might dine at his table.

After we had rested we were given a late lunch in our room and by the time all this was over it was time to depart for the docks, and our freighter. Together with all our luggage we took the inevitable taxi ride and eventually found the *Mormactrade*, a vessel which was making a 'run' between New York and Argentina.

As we were about to embark we were approached by the purser who informed us the Captain had gone ashore and was not expected to return until quite late, since we would not be leaving until the following morning.

Further, we were told, 'You cannot take those cats aboard. They will go in the hold.' This was an unfortunate reception, most of all for Fifi, for whom this kind of treatment was all too common.

The Guv brought out his letter from the ship's company

18

confirming we had permission to have Fifi and Ku'ei in our suite. By this time the Guv was becoming very tired of the situation and he told the Purser, 'If they cannot be with us then we will not go either.' At last we had our way, being told it could all be sorted out in the morning with the Captain. We thought of cancelling the whole trip and I believe it would have been better if we had done so – but we didn't. Later we heard that no instructions had been left regarding treatment of the Cat People but it was too late, Fifi had suffered another shock at the hands of humanity.

From our stateroom, just aft the bridge, we watched while two locomotives were put on deck – they were huge contraptions with extremely powerful propulsion units – their destination being Brazil. Next morning brought great activity aboardship and, as we watched from a position near the bridge, harbour tugs chugged along and drew the *Mormactrade* out, backwards. Then changing position, they approached the bow, and towed us forward into the waters of New York Harbour.

On we went, past all the great liners which were docked, past the Statue of Liberty, up beneath a bridge, when soon the Ambrose Lightship came in sight. We waved a greeting to some of the men aboard and then we turned to the right – South.

Before finally leaving the United States behind us, we had one port of call, Charleston, on the coast of South Carolina. Here we docked for one day so I went out to look at the town, and the stores, returning with an armful of periodicals to keep us interested during the coming days. Also a pair of nice beige shoes in readiness for the summer days in Uruguay. The seasons being reversed we would arrive in South America around mid-summer.

The Guv has always enjoyed sea travel but, like Fifi, I prefer to stay in one place; if I HAVE to go anywhere let it be by air and get it over with, let me arrive at my destination as quickly as possible. Now, a row-boat on the river is fine for an hour's pleasure, or a boat fitted with an outboard motor such as we used in Ireland; that is different but a longish sea trip, no!

It must have been on our first morning on the *Mormactrade* – after we set sail, that is, when I awoke around five o'clock to find Mrs Fifi right beside me, not saying a word but obviously waiting for her breakfast. 'All right,' I told her. 'Here goes – you will have your breakfast in a few minutes.' As I collected myself and stood up, suddenly I felt everything inside me reverse and I remember thinking, 'Ah, this is it, the start of seasickness about which I have been warned.' Somehow food was placed before Greywhiskers and then I had to lie down while the Guv brought me some anti-sickness pills – I do not remember clearly exactly what, but they certainly were effective.

By the time a day had passed I had recovered from the attack. Then a storm – one of the worst – overcame us as we made our way along the US coast, in the Cape Hatteras area, which is never calm in the winter months. It was reported to be the biggest storm in years, with many ships scurrying towards the safety of a harbour, but cargo ships must take all risks since the chief concern is PROFIT. There is no time for delays.

The vessel battled on against immense waves and at one point there was no other alternative but to pull into harbour, because the cargo in the aft hold had been damaged, and certain volatile liquids had escaped and were sloshing around in the bottom of the hold. That was soon pumped out and on she went once more.

Our suitcases and other objects in our suite slid across the floor during the night and Miss Ku'ei didn't seem to mind at all, even when the chair upon which she had been

20

sleeping joined in the dance. It was a different situation for Mrs Greywhiskers, who was older and quite frail; Fifi just stayed in her place becoming more and more quiet and one night I watched over her, while the Guv soothed her spirit, but sad to relate she did not recover. Towards morning she lifted her head as if to say 'I am going now', and so she left us to join Mr T. Catt and Miss Sindhi.

Each time a Cat Person leaves us it is never any easier for those who are left behind. So Fifi found her last earthly resting place in the raging waters of the US coastline. Now she is well and contented, continuing her evolution in another sphere.

The Captain was most helpful and understanding; his men performed the last rites for our much loved Fifi, and the loss was documented in the ship's log.

The most wonderful thing
is that you and I
are always walking together,
hand in hand,
in a strangely beautiful world,
unknown to other people.
We both stretch one hand
to receive from Life –
and Life is generous indeed.

Kahlil Gibran

FOUR

We noticed how the water was polluted with sewage, refuse, anything, but as we continued further out into the Atlantic the sea became clearer and clearer.

Once we saw a great bomber overhead – it seemed to be a vast aircraft as it swooped down towards us, passing above the deck at just a few hundred feet. 'Giving us a check over,' commented the Captain, at our side. 'They're afraid we might be Russians taking supplies to Castro.' As we all knew Fidel Castro had been defying the USA and arousing their ire. The Russians had been trying to place Atom bombs, or something, on Cuba as a threat to the USA. The American plane, satisfied that we were innocent traders went off; again the sea was deserted. Cuba was just across to our right, down below the horizon.

I had planned to re-read the manuscript of *Living with the Lama*, which had not yet been published but, after Fifi departed, I could not bring myself to open the pages so I waited until it was in book form. Fifi's book, written by

Lobsang Rampa, is one of the most popular of the series.

So we continued and at last the arrangement of the clouds, just above the skyline, indicated that land was beneath. 'The loom of the land,' the Captain said, 'You always get different clouds above land to what you do above the sea.'

On we went, eventually crossing the equator but without those ceremonies which some ships have, where passengers are subjected to treatment by the 'Gods of the Sea', to celebrate the event. This of course if it is your first crossing. We had no time for such frivolities, this was a ship of commerce, the *Mormactrade*, although the crew teased us and would have liked to give us a dunking.

One of the officers was a great talker, to whoever would listen, and his favourite subject was his wife. He kept saying, 'She spends money like it was going out of fashion.' It was the first time I had heard that remark, but not the last. If we needed to send a cable we had to go up to see the Radio Operator; to anyone interested he would explain the intricacies of his job, a job which makes for a somewhat lonely life. A bigger ship would carry two radio operators but there was only one on the *Mormactrade*, which meant his being on duty for twenty-four hours a day, even sleeping on the job so that no calls would be missed.

There was much excitement when the news was announced that soon we would be making our first South American port of call; we looked forward with pleasure to being able to walk on land once more.

Each time we came close to a port we were able to receive radio programmes from that particular town or city, otherwise we relied on the short-waves, when it was possible to get news from various parts of the world. One advantage of ocean travel is the ease with which one can receive non-interference radio reception.

So we were about to visit the Brazilian port of Vitória,

23

after turning into the wide mouth of a river, and passing an island which seemed to be a mighty rock, to our port side.

At the Vitória docks, amid much noise and confusion, clinking of engines and rattling of chains, our two locomotives were unloaded; they were lifted up by the ship's derricks and placed on the tracks running from the dock. It was interesting to see how first of all the bogeys and other wheels were placed in position and wedged, so that they were unable to move, then the body of the loco, the engine proper, was carefully lowered on the wheel arrangement. Quicker than seemed possible the locomotives were started and went away beyond our sight.

With all that weight removed the ship was steadier; less of the rolling, less pitch and toss – a forward and backward motion which was quite sickening.

Soon the remainder of the cargo was disposed of and then the *Mormactrade* turned and steamed away again, down the river, to continue South, and fairly close to land where we could see various activities. We saw battered cars on the roads, cars held together with baling wire, and rope. Then we passed the great port of Rio de Janeiro but we did not stop there, this trip being to Argentina and Uruguay.

A nice sitting room was available to the passengers, so sometimes we sat there after scanning the ship's library, finding a book to while away the time. Miss Ku'ei enjoyed it, especially if there was someone to talk to her, for she had been lonely without Fifi Greywhiskers. Whenever the Captain came around he enjoyed a chat with the Guv, and he was a most agreeable gentleman who had a pleasant greeting for everyone. Life can be lonely for the Master, or Captain of a ship and it is not surprising that he is allowed to take his wife along when he so desires. The Captain of the *Mormactrade* had his wife with him at the start of the trip but she stayed only a few days, after which she returned to the USA. During the time of the storm she was very helpful, frequently visiting her husband when he refused to leave the Bridge until the worst was over.

It was disappointing for us not to be stopping in the port of Rio de Janeiro, but there was nothing we could do about it so we hoped that perhaps another time! The Captain informed us that the *Mormactrade* would call at Rio on the return voyage.

It was intended we would be taken to Uruguay, where we would disembark at Montevideo, cargo would be unloaded and then the *Mormactrade* would continue on to Buenos Aires, the end of the voyage. In front of us was the city of Punta del Este, with its sparkling beaches and shining dwellings, that 'point to the east' which always reminds me of the Great Train Robbery of Great Britain. Several of the fugitive robbers, fled to Punta del Este where they settled down to enjoy the fruits of their loot. At any rate many people of Montevideo spent vacations in that healthy and select area, where those who could afford the luxury, owned a second home, an apartment or a house. A lovely and desirable place for spending a holiday.

So we continued, with Montevideo in view, expecting that soon we would reach our destination, and feeling somewhat thankful that our trip was nearly over. However, as we approached the harbour we came to a halt – it was absolutely crowded with vessels of all nations and, if we had docked, we might have had to wait for a week or more before unloading. Because of a strike by stevedores everything was at a standstill, so the Captain decided he would have to go on to Argentina first, having a special cargo for that country and feeling it would be futile to wait.

What a nuisance for him – would he ever get rid of those passengers for Uruguay?

Those who cannot remember the past are condemned to repeat it.

George Santayana

FIVE

The Guv and Miss Ku'ei appeared to be enjoying themselves so they would not mind the extra travelling time, and really there was no cause for concern since we would get a glimpse of Buenos Aires which otherwise we would have missed.

We passed the lightship in the Rio de la Plata, at the junction of the sea lane leading to Montevideo and Buenos Aires, and continued on. Later our minds would be refreshed regarding an important event which had occurred in this river which I had previously known as the River Plate. By the following morning we were actually in the land mass of Argentina. Buenos Aires has a very large volume of sea traffic, and this was no exception, many ships were entering the port, and many leaving, as we arrived.

Our stay lasted a few days, which gave one the opportunity to visit down town and the first place I wanted to find was a bookstore. There were plenty of taxis to be had by the docks so I was quickly whisked away to what I was told was one of the main book suppliers. Here I found titles in English, not knowing any Spanish in those days and even now I doubt whether I could master a book in that language. After making a few other purchases I returned to the ship with plenty of reading material, fresh radio batteries and, of course, fruit and chocolates.

On the morning after our arrival there was much excitement in the air – it was reported that an unidentified flying object had been seen in the vicinity of the airport, and that event was the main subject of conversation for some time. Those who are interested will probably be aware that South America is a popular place for UFO sightings, especially Argentina and Brazil. Some people are reported to have been taken aboard by the craft's occupants.

Not to be outdone I might add that here in Alberta we have not been forgotten; especially in the past few years there have been an increasing number of sightings, reported by most reliable witnesses such as police and air pilots. I wonder, sometimes, if they are following us around!

At last we were ready for the last lap of our journey and the Captain cheerily remarked, 'We'll soon have you in Montevideo. It's not such a delay as I feared.' And then he added, 'By the way you know "Montevideo" means "I see a mountain", because you should know that before you arrive.'

The Captain also reminded us that the correct designation of the country we were visiting is Uruguay del Oriental, with emphasis on the 'al', something we already knew. Or was it the other way around – Oriental del Uruguay!

The ship was turned again and we headed seaward down the river Plate with its great sandbanks, its silt-choked waters which were the graveyard of many ships which had failed to navigate the passage and had got stuck in the mud. On we went, through the night until we had a lightship on our port side, and, as we came to a near-stop a pilot came aboard to direct us into the harbour. The river bed was absolutely silted due to the water channel varying from day to day. With the pilot on the Bridge, still there was no respite for the Captain because, although apparently the pilot was in charge, the unfortunate Captain would be held

27

responsible should an accident occur. The Captain's *chief* function, I am told, is to keep the vessel afloat.

Leaving the lightship we turned into the channel leading to the port of Montevideo and, with bare steerage way, the *Mormactrade* ambled towards the port. The Captain hove in view. 'There's no point in hurrying,' he said. 'The strike is over, but the harbour is still full of vessels and we are the last one in.'

So we decided we had better settle down for another wait and, in the meantime, we took stock of the surrounding activity. On the left we espied a ship-wreck – with only the upper works protruding above the surface of the water, the masts a tangle of rigging. Lifeboats were smashed and in all the parts visible, there was only one piece of glass unbroken.

The Captain was only too pleased to enlighten us as to the wreck's history; he must have told the story many times but that is a part of a sea captain's life, for many are the tales he can relate, often improved in the telling. 'It's a very sad case,' we were told. 'It was a passenger liner and due for inspection at Lloyds but it had many defects, a great deal was wrong with it which meant a lower rating, less profitable. So, somehow the sea cocks were opened and the bilges began to fill with water.' He looked rueful as he continued, 'The captain ran her straight up on the sandbanks, and there she'll stay until the last bit of metal has rusted. She's so full of sand and it would cost more to salvage her than the ship is worth.'

Again the captain talked, as though in a reverie, 'The local fishermen bless the ship because it attracts a lot of fish. Fish always go for wrecks, you know, and this one is an absolute harvest for fishermen.' As it was low tide we could see the ship clearly, the outline of the main deck, the rails around the main deck, and the hatches over the hold.

'Some people have landed on it, you know,' said the Captain. 'People have been aboard and they've taken just about everything they could reach. The ship's clock, the ship's bell, there's only one lifeboat left, and it is staved in on the far side, so it's just left there.' The ship was *The Highland Monarch*!

We drifted along, the *Mormactrade* under perfect control, notwithstanding the slow speed, and viewed this veritable graveyard in the estuary, and we were dismayed as the Captain kept reminding us that we would have to stay around until all the other vessels had been dealt with first. When you travel by freighter you cannot guarantee within a day or two when you will arrive or depart from a port, unlike a passenger ship which is more punctual. It is never certain how long it will take to unload various cargo so when one travels by this method it is no use having plans which you cannot change – better to go by air.

A ship's captain must be one of the most interesting persons to meet, for various reasons – he is usually an excellent story teller and he is, mostly, a philosophical person, not having to worry about day to day problems which beset those in cities and offices. He has more time to think and to dwell on the realities of life – yes, and death.

To keep us interested the Captain of *Mormactrade* pointed to a place between us and the shore remarking, 'The *Graf Spee* went down there, you know.' There to our left and just ahead, was the grave of the *Graf Spee*, a pocket battleship, a commerce-raider, a ship of Hitler's Germany, which had become famous in World War Two. And now Nemesis had taken the ship. There had been a running battle at sea, outside the port, and the captain of the battleship, Captain Langsdorff, had been misled by British signals which were intended to mislead him. He had already received a pounding from a small cruiser and some destroyers, and he expected further attack by destroyers. So he made for the Port of Montevideo to have the ship patched and have fresh ammunition and fuel put aboard.

According to the International Rules of War, a warship could put into a neutral port only for seventy-two hours, otherwise it would be deemed to be giving aid and comfort to the enemy, and could be shelled. So, after the allotted time had elapsed, the battleship was compelled to leave and there was much speculation at the thousands of men who were left ashore.

Captain Langsdorff said he was going to make a fast run to Germany and, without all those men the ship would travel all the faster! ! ! So the *Graf Spee* left port but, instead of entering the channel leading to the sea, it turned right as though it were intending to go to Buenos Aires. But no! Out of port she dropped anchor in the sandbanks, and men were seen leaving the battleship, using their own lifeboats, tugs, anything which would float.

With the last man gone, there was a terrific explosion which shattered windows in the city of Montevideo. The whole superstructure of the *Graf Spee* lifted clear of the decks and dropped down again. The ship was ablaze from stem to stern. The captain, a brave man and a courteous foe, was taken ashore to Montevideo and interrogated extensively. He said he was merely following Hitler's order, 'Scuttle, let not the ship be captured. Scuttle.' So he'd followed the orders and scuttled the ship. Then after giving assurance that he would not attempt to escape Captain Langsdorff was allowed to retire to his hotel. Soon afterwards a single shot was heard and Captain Langsdorff had taken his own life.

Here lies a most beautiful lady,
Light of step and heart was she
I think she was the most beautiful lady
That ever was in the West Country.
Her beauty vanishes; beauty passes;
However rare, rare it be;
And when I crumble who shall remember
this lady of the West Country?

Walter de la Mare.

SIX

Mr U had been keeping contact with the *Mormactrade*, eager to know how soon we might be expected to disembark, and one day we were notified that he had been given permission to visit us on board ship. The next day a party of six or seven persons arrived and they were all introduced by Mr U – an interesting group, including a musician and a lawyer. Also Mr U had bought his wife along, a most attractive and intelligent lady.

Mostly the discussion was woven around the Guv and his books, and the plans they had for lectures to groups of interested persons, and hopes that he would accept individual students.

Eventually the conversation got around to immediate needs, where we would live, who would show us around etcetera. We were told that a house had been rented, some twelve miles from the city, in a residential district not far from the airport. We found later that it was a most desirable area for those who had a means of transport to the city, for shopping or sightseeing, but we were to find Carrasco too isolated.

At last came the time to bid the Captain goodbye, and we were taken in Mr U's car to our new home. He took the route along the Rambla so that we might enjoy the beauties of Montevideo, although we would have preferred the shorter way, being anxious to get to our house and settle in. Mr U's wife and the musician were in the car ahead of us, with some of our luggage and they kept saying they must hurry because they had 'a mission'. When eventually we caught up with them they were out of the car and holding a banner right across the entrance to the property. To our amusement and some pleasure we read, 'WELCOME LOBSANG RAMPA.' The musician had a keen sense of humour, even if it seemed perverted at times. One day he tried to make us say to another person, 'You are my *enemigo*', so that he might enjoy the joke, but we were not trapped even though our Spanish was very limited in the early days. You cannot go 'round telling people they are your enemy!

The house was all on one level, with three bedrooms, and a garden at front and rear, and it was in the bathroom of this house where we came face to face with Mr Frog as mentioned in *Pussywillow*. We had been aboard ship for approximately twenty-three days so we were installed in our new home just two days before Christmas, in the middle of summer. What a change after being used to the cold of winter, and snow, and it was the quietest holiday season I had ever spent, Mr U. having arranged to visit relatives some miles distant.

Fortunately we soon met a young family who lived nearby, and we appreciated the fact that the wife spoke English, being the daughter of an Englishman. She found the association agreeable, giving her the opportunity to broaden her vocabulary and learn more about England, which she had never visited. Even now this English lady is remembered, especially when we have occasion to use a tape-recorder – she had never used such an instrument before so she found it quite a novelty. When the Guv let her hear herself on tape she looked astonished for a few seconds then smiling, 'I *like* my voice', she said. We particularly remember this incident in view of the remarks of most people who, on hearing a playback, will say, 'Is that my voice. No, it can't be. I don't sound like that.'

We stayed only five weeks in that house while searching for something more suitable nearer, or in, the city.

The area suffered many dust-storms and one would find the floor covered with a fine dust – the wind just swept along the open spaces in Carrasco and those storms were extremely unpleasant; Uruguay has too few trees thus causing this situation, reminding one of the dustbowls of North America.

Following the Christmas holidays I took a trip into Montevideo with the idea of doing a bit of shopping and looking for an apartment, but not very hopeful of achieving the latter. However, on the return journey I noticed a big apartment building on the Rambla, at a point named Punta Carreta, so I went up to have a closer look. There was a 'for rent' sign listed so I made a note of the address, and apartment number, and continued my taxi journey home to report to the Guv.

Nothing is ever arranged quickly in Uruguay so there was no way we could hurry anyone. The English lady volunteered to go with me to view the property; she loved change so it was a pleasure for her to accompany me. We arranged a day and time suitable for her, and off we went, hoping we would find someone at home. Pressing the intercom buzzer, soon a voice answered, in Spanish, so my companion stated our business, whereupon we were asked to come in and the door-release was activated. On arrival at the apartment we found the gentleman at home, with his wife and child, and they said they were leaving 'to take up residence in Argentina'. The accommodation was very satisfactory, with its living room facing the river, and balcony extending from the living room to two bedrooms.

There was little one could do until Mr U had been contacted, since he was acting as sponsor, on behalf of the group which had brought us to their country. So, among other things I learned something of real estate procedure when we went to a bank where the contract was executed. It seemed very strange to me after being used to dealing with an estate agent, in England, or a real-estate officer (who needs special training) in Canada. However the transaction was completed at last and we moved in Bel Horizon in the early days of February.

A great improvement, with only one floor above us, we could look right out to the mouth of the river Plate, to where it flowed into the Atlantic, and we needed only to step outside to find a store or two, which was very convenient. There were other apartment buildings but none quite close so we were able to breathe comfortably. On one side was a vacant space, probably being kept ready for a construction company to take over – and by this time we were feeling more settled, having to some extent 'found our bearings'.

If I had been shopping or taking care of other business in what is known as the old part of Montevideo, in the banking district, and near the docks, I would return home, after securing a taxi, by the Rambla, enjoying the river and avoiding the city traffic. To this day I can, and sometimes do, visualize that tall building in the distance where I would feast my eyes, thinking. 'Up there, in the second apartment from the top is MY FAMILY, which means more to me than anything in the world.' I picture the Guv, sitting on the balcony, and Miss Ku'ei who shared all my waking, and sleeping, moments, sitting by the door five minutes before I was due, so that she might welcome her Ma. Ku'ei, who is no longer around physically, but definitely with us in another form.

Mr U often came to visit us, and we would sit in the large living room, or on the balcony, watching the glorious sunsets, while chatting on all kinds of topics. Mr U had quite a sense of humour, never minding if someone made him the butt of a joke. Once the Guv had a tiny battery in his hand, having pretended to remove it from his ear. 'What is that?' enquired our visitor. 'Oh,' answered the Guv. 'That is the battery which makes me go.' For a moment Mr U seemed stunned and then, rocking in his chair, he burst out laughing. 'You were so convincing,' he said, 'that I almost believed you.'

The latter part of a wise man's life
is taken up in curing the follies,
prejudices, and false opinions
he had contracted in the former.

Jonathan Swift

BLUE GREY

'Oh, look,' I said when we were sitting in the hall one day.
'What a pitiful little creature over there.' The janitor, standing nearby, indicated that he had found the tiny kitten in
the vacant lot adjoining our building. It was the only one
left of a litter, and he had taken pity on it, and brought it
in.

Juan, the janitor, was fairly young, perhaps thirty and,
with his wife, he had come from Paraguay. Often he might
be seen in front of our apartment building, busy washing
tenants' cars, usually in bare feet. The climate in Uruguay
is very temperate, never very cold, although the residents
would have a different opinion if you asked them how they
felt around July, the middle of winter. Anyhow it was so
beautiful that Juan needed no shoes when he performed this
particular duty, and the way he splashed around with the
hose meant that he would only have ruined his shoes anyhow.

The little grey kitten fascinated me and I wondered why
it looked so bedraggled, as it sat there, at the far end of the
large lobby, never moving. Eventually I learned that for
purposes of hygiene Juan had decided to clean the little
cat and what had he used to do it – but kerosene. I also
learned that he was caring for the tiny creature, where he
had placed a carton for it, in the boiler room.

Of course it was dark down there, this room being on a lower level, *and hot*. The poor little cat was so pleased when someone visited her and one hated leaving her down there, while outside the sun shone and a lovely breeze made one feel just right. I felt it was wrong to be enjoying a free life when a little person was imprisoned in such surroundings.

What to do about the situation? Discuss it with the Guv, of course. After that consult Miss Ku'ei who, through the circumstance of her birth, was possessed of a strongly possessive trait, together with the fact that she was of the Siamese family who prefer to be 'one person' cats. I have mentioned her birth month in my first book, *Pussywillow*, so I will not labour the point, except to comment that her birthday was a national holiday in Uruguay.

In the end we decided to tell Juan we were prepared to take the kitten, and see what could be done for her, how she would respond to living with a human family, and whether Ku'ei would adjust to sharing her life. Ku'ei had become accustomed to managing without Fifi but we knew she sometimes felt lonesome. Fifi had been a mature person, and quiet, as well as being a Siamese, but this was different – a so-called domestic cat, still only a baby who might annoy Ku'ei who was, even then, quite mature. Would the cat adjust to an indoor life? That, also, was something to be considered.

Blue Grey, as we called her, because of her colouring which we could distinguish after cleaning off all the kerosene, when brought up to our apartment, was naturally very nervous. Fortunately there was one room which she could call her own – it had two doors, one leading into the kitchen and the other joined the passage to the bedroom area. It had been used as a dining room but was suitable for sleeping, with its own 'half-bath' as we call it here in Canada, so Blue Grey would have all amenities. We had provided

37

food when she was in the boiler room so she would soon get used to a constant wholesome diet, and we had great hopes for her.

After a few days it was noticed that the little cat was not very steady on her feet, she did not seem to be gaining strength so a veterinarian was summoned. He confirmed our suspicions that she had been starved in her early days, and all we could do was to continue giving nourishing food. He prescribed vitamins and calcium, observing her progress in the hope that the condition would be overcome. I spent a lot of time with her, and she purred loudly whenever she received attention.

The young veterinarian visited several times, sometimes hopeful and other times not so hopeful. Eventually, at our request as to whether she would get better, he said that after observing her closely during his visits he doubted there would ever be any improvement, that the mother had most likely been starved too, before Blue Grey was born, so the poor little kitten never had a chance.

There was no use in blinding ourselves to the situation and the young vet had never been too optimistic about the success of his treatment. Little Blue Grey would never be healthy, would never be able to walk properly and we were advised to have her sent Home. It was a sad decision to make, but by far the best for the little cat, so the veterinarian gave her an injection, painlessly, and she slept away her young life.

Juan lovingly prepared a resting place at the back of our building, not far from the spot where, just a few weeks earlier, he had found her. A decade and a half later I can still see clearly the small form, wrapped in my dressing gown, being taken down in the elevator. 'Goodbye, little cat,' I thought. 'Perhaps you will come to me again.' My Autumn lady!

38

In order to maintain a well-balanced perspective
the person who has a dog to worship him
should have a cat to ignore him.

SEVEN

In a short time the Friends of Lobsang Rampa had formed
a discussion group, based on the author's books, and once
or twice each month they would put together a list of
questions regarding something which, in their opinion, required further clarification. Since Lobsang Rampa has never
been completely in favour of group study, believing one can
make better progress on one's own, he was not anxious to
attend the sessions. However he compromised with the
members by putting the answers to queries on tape and,
periodically, he would record some new material.

Most of the members were men but the group included
several women, and it was good to see how much the Guv
was appreciated; he would receive appreciative messages
in the way of letters and various other gestures.

Of those interested in having Lobsang Rampa in their
country was a previous president, and this we found en-
couraging. At that time the government was composed of
a nine man council, each member of the council in power
taking his turn and being President for one year. The particular gentleman was at the time seriously ill and confined
in a hospital bed. At his request it was intended that he
would meet the Guv and there was a discussion as to which
of the two people would effect the introduction. Since
both persons could not do this, and they could not agree
between them, nothing came of the visit, and in the mean-

time the patient was not improving so there was disappointment on both sides.

A delightful lady lived in our building and she was a descendant of a rather important French general. Married to a surgeon, she was rather plump and even tempered – like me (I hope). She enjoyed meeting different people and sometimes I would take Miss Ku'ei to visit the French lady, in the later afternoon. Sensibly the Señora indulged in a little siesta so that she would feel fresh in the evening; it seemed to be a very satisfactory way of life. This lady kept in touch with us during the remainder of our stay, even when we moved away from Bel Horizon.

In the apartment above us there lived a gentleman, a Consul from a European country, and he must have done a fair amount of entertaining, judging by the loud noise emanating from that direction. We never knew him personally, but we certainly knew of his existence.

Although our stay in Uruguay lasted little more than two years we experienced life in three different establishments, and the third apartment provided more of the 'home' atmosphere, being smaller and more friendly.

We had seen an advertisement in the daily newspaper where an individual had two dwellings for rent, or so it seemed. When we contacted the advertiser by telephone it appeared she was an agent and she was handling rentals for two separate people. After looking over the first we decided it would be quite adequate for our needs, it was furnished and more centrally located, so we advised the agent of our decision.

Somehow there was a misunderstanding, the agent became difficult so we told her she could find another tenant, we were giving it up.

About an hour after returning home to Bel Horizon a lady arrived to the door, appearing somewhat agitated and saying she must talk to us. She was a charming person, another French lady, who said she, or rather her son, owned the apartment in Calle Constituente, and she understood we were interested in renting the premises. She said she was familiar with the works of Lobsang Rampa and nothing would give her greater pleasure than having the Rampa family as tenants. It was a pleasant association and at last we began to feel less strange in another country. We would move in at the beginning of March, just as the year at Bel Horizon came to an end, and each month I would go by bus to the house of the French family to take our monthly cheque, and stay for a friendly chat before returning home. Of course the landlord would have collected the dues or we could have used the mail, except the postal service was not always reliable, but I enjoyed the short trip to Francesco Soca.

It was definitely an improvement, this Constituente address, for we were able to get into the city centre more easily, especially since the bus service was excellent and to use a common present day phrase we were more 'our own people'. Miss Ku'ei enjoyed the change, especially her trips to the roof of the building, where I would take her each day. She would sit by the door just after lunch, and wait for me and if, for any reason, I couldn't go she was most displeased.

One of the most vivid memories I have regarding that apartment was of a person who visited me, a person who had performed a few services for us, such as translations etcetera. A delightful personality, with a sense of humour, though not intended when she enquired, 'Is your husband tame?' I was highly amused, until I realized what she meant. 'Oh, yes,' I answered. 'He is a fairly quiet person.' Then I explained that my cat was tame but not my husband.

Many of the dwellings in Montevideo had flat roofs and

41

these were utilized to the greatest advantage. Some people kept poultry up there and I will never forget the day we suffered a severe windstorm, more accurately a hurricane, when a number of chickens were swept from one roof over to another, right across an open space. I think the Guv has mentioned the incident in one of his books. Something else seemed strange to us and that was the sight of a dog on top of a house – on thinking about it the dog was probably much safer than if it was just running around on the street. But if it was hungry, and suffering from extreme heat, or cold, one felt sympathetic towards the creature. I have seen a thin, unhappy dog just pacing up and down in its misery.

I do not see how we can criticize another country for its apparent carelessness towards pets, and animals in general, when here in privileged Canada we are as uncaring as anywhere in the world – with of course *some* exceptions. Take for example certain incidents which occur during the summer holiday season in this province of Alberta, where too many people seem more concerned with their own pleasures than with responsibility towards their so-called pets. Some six months ago, on a Canadian national holiday, many were the reports of animals being thrown from automobiles and just left to the mercies of fast-driven vehicles, to predators of the wild or, at least, just left to starve. A strange way to treat man's so-called 'best friend', the dog, who places his whole trust in his master or mistress, often to become the victim of the worst kind of treachery.

One dog was reported found with its leg tied around its neck to prevent it from walking – the reason for such action must be beyond the comprehension of right thinking persons.

About sixty dogs were found abandoned on the road to Banff National Park and the authorities were able to save only a fraction of their number, pointing out that those

42

persons who are tired of keeping their pets, or who find it too inconvenient to continue caring, should take the animal to the 'pound' where, if other homes cannot be found, they will not suffer if they have to be sent Home. Too many people seem to think that by just abandoning a dog or a cat *SOMEONE* will find it and take it home, but this is not what happens as those individuals would realize if *THEY* were suddenly dumped in a strange place, far from their homes, with no means of survival. I often wonder, too, how humans would enjoy being hunted, just as fox-hunting is tolerated in England, where one would imagine the population to be a little more civilized than are some of us Canadians.

Cruelty has a human heart
And Jealousy a human face;
Terror the human form divine,
And Secrecy the human dress.

William Blake,
From 'A Divine Image'.

EIGHT

In North America there has been a lot of fuss, and rightly so, about the dumping of poisonous chemicals in the water at Niagara Falls and many other places in the USA. Tests have been made on animals to see the extent of the danger so that humans may benefit – and the media was quoted as saying, 'No one in their right mind would think of making the tests on humans.'

All right, if animals are expected to suffer on our behalf, the least we can do is to make them as comfortable as possible and not just go round 'shooting indiscriminately', or otherwise harassing the creatures of nature who, but for various religions which teach us that only man has a soul, we would accept as equals.

In the name of sport we have hunters chasing a herd of elk out of a National Park while, in a state of panic, they all bunch together, obviously suffering from stress, the hunter waiting for an animal to 'make a break', his excitement causing his aim to be erratic and half the time just injuring but not killing the animal outright. One elk was reported to be suffering so much stress that it walked a few steps, stopped and just fell down dead, without being shot. Later many injured animals were found, having made their

44

way back into the park, the remainder of the herd completely disorganized and disoriented.

What about the other side of the picture? How do animals treat the human race? The other day a dog saved the life of a four-year-old child who was drowning in a creek – he swam out to the child who climbed on the dog's back and was brought to safety. And a cat alerted the family when their home was on fire thus saving all their lives.

Dolphins Save Men's Lives. One of the nicest stories comes from Belleville, South Africa, reported in the *Calgary Herald*, December 1978. Because of the great interest in dolphins and the efforts which have been made to communicate with them, I will here repeat the story:

Four fishermen say they were saved from certain death at sea by four dolphins. The magazine *South African Panorama* reports that after the men had lost their way the dolphins came to the rescue, forcing their boat away from the rocky coast and leading it to a safe harbour.

'It was the most frightening and incredible experience I've ever had,' says fisherman Kobus Stander. 'We were completely lost. The mist was terribly thick. Unknowingly we were steering straight towards the rocks when the dolphins turned up.'

Two other men, who were in the boat with Stander and his son Barend, were quoted as saying they regarded the incident as miraculous. They were fishing for barracuda when, at about 1 pm they were enveloped in a thick mist.

'We immediately weighed anchor and started moving towards Dessen Island,' Stander says. 'The mist thickened so quickly we could barely see beyond two metres. Twenty minutes later we were completely lost. We began to feel panicky.'

One of the other men, Mac Macgregor, went to the bow, trying to peer through the mist. Suddenly he felt a bump on the right-hand side and, looking over, he saw two dolphins. The dolphins forced the boat to the left where two others were swimming.

'I realized the dolphins' odd behaviour could be significant and shouted to Stander to steer to the left. Stander pulled the tiller round wildly, and we just managed to graze past the rocks.' Other than the dolphins, nothing could be seen in the fog.

'We did not have the slightest clue where we were,' said the third man, W. W. Matthee. 'The two dolphins on the right-hand side kept forcing the bow towards the left.' Moments later they narrowly missed rocks on the right-hand side. 'I was getting a strange feeling that we ought to leave our destiny to the dolphins,' said Stander, 'since it was clear they had twice prevented us from running on to the rocks.'

The men followed the dolphins for another thirty minutes, but still could not make out where they were going.

'After a while the dolphins stopped swimming at the front of the boat. All four started circling around the boat,' said Macgregor. 'We asked Stander to reduce speed, saw that we were now in calm water and dropped anchor. The dolphins kept playing around the boat for a while and then disappeared into the thick mist.'

Said Stander, 'When the mist cleared and the houses of Ysterfontein could be discerned, we were speechless. We had intended going ashore at Dessen Island. We had never dreamed the dolphins would guide us to Ysterfontein.'

Better do a kindness near home
than go far away to burn incense.

Chinese proverb

NINE

Fortunately Miss Ku'ei and I had the use of a short-wave
radio in those days and, for someone not fluent in Spanish,
it helped us to keep in touch with the world. Mostly we
tuned in to the BBC or to stations in North America, and
we spent many hours listening to musical programmes, and
to the news. We were astonished one evening when suddenly there came the announcement that Nikita Khrushchev
of Russia had been ousted while he was out of the country,
although it should have caused no surprise since that is the
way things are done in that country.

It was an eventful year in world affairs and I was reminded of this as I listened last night to the CBC programme *As It Happens* with the popular hostess Barbara
Frum. There was the voice of Lyndon Johnson who had
become President the previous year, after the assassination
of John Kennedy, and one heard Martin Luther King
speaking out on the civil rights problem; the British government was having trouble; and it was the year of the Beatles.
It seemed something of a coincidence, and a welcome one,
that I should tune in to the programme just as I had reached
that era in my story.

I have mentioned in one of my previous books there was
a period when we were just 'kicking our heels' – a strike at
the docks which meant a hold up of periodicals, etcetera,
and, apart from a few books, we had nothing to read in

English. The Guv decided it would be a suitable opportunity to write something himself, thus *The Saffron Robe* came about. The title was one we had thought of when *The Third Eye* was being written. If a title can help in making a book popular, then *The Third Eye* was an excellent choice – it must have sold a million copies or more.

One day we had a visitor in the form of an author's agent who came over from Argentina. This gentleman stayed the afternoon, having tea with us, and I still remember how he liked it – with lemon. Since that time I have come to know him better for now he handles my books in Spanish and he has given me a great deal of encouragement. I am sure he will recognize himself!

Just recently I have been reading a book which deals with authors, author's agents, editors and publishers and I have come to the conclusion that I am extremely fortunate in having such helpful publishers and agents in four countries. As well as in England and Argentina, my books are published in Brazil and French Canada.

One day one of the *amigos* brought along a friend to meet Lobsang Rampa, to see whether the friend could be helped in the matter of constant headaches, and a general feeling of tiredness. The lady was also accompanied by her husband, and together they hoped for a miracle to happen. Well, the Guv listened, and observed, and decided the condition could be alleviated, so with the confidence of this person, coupled with the Guv's acknowledged healing powers, the friend of the *amigo* soon felt very much improved. Anyone familiar with the practice of transmitting healing to another person will know that it takes a great deal of energy, on the part of the practitioner, so one hopes the patient will treat the matter in all seriousness.

It was obvious this lady was suffering, she kept reminding

us of the fact with her frequent mutterings, 'Yo sufrir mucho' but what did she do on that same Saturday night after being rid of her pain and discomfort? Because she felt so well and so happy she and her husband went partying, and danced for half the night. The following day she did not feel so well, naturally, and *we* did not feel too good about it either. It had been only a friendly gesture on the part of the Guv with, of course, no fee involved, and he would have been justified in believing he had wasted his time and talents!

Again, on a Saturday, a group of about twelve persons came to have a discussion in our apartment, some of *los amigos* of Montevideo, and the remainder had come from Buenos Aires. The doorman must have been startled when all those people arrived; he must have wondered how we expected to cope in such a small space. The living room was tiny, it was also the bedroom of Miss Ku'ei and me, but we managed to squeeze everybody in – some sitting on the bed, others had chairs, and some made do with the floor.

We all enjoyed the 'meeting' but it was hard on the Guv. Someone would ask a question, it would be passed on by one who acted as interpreter, and the Guv would have the answer relayed in the same way. Oh, yes! It was most interesting. One can learn a great deal by listening to others' conversations, except most of us prefer to talk rather than listen.

Many of the subjects dealt with have since appeared in later books by Lobsang Rampa so I will not task the reader's patience by repetition.

As I write this, however, I am reminded of a remark someone passed the other day. The discussion was on a popular subject of the moment, that of life and death, and it was put to me that perhaps the after-life would prove to

49

be no better than this present life on earth. 'You can't be sure,' it was suggested, 'that when you get to the other side of life you won't find there is still another stage, higher, which you will yearn for.' I looked at my companion, who continued, 'You can't be sure of anything so it is better to believe in this life while you are here, and not count on anything after.'

Well, I thought about the matter, and it all seemed so simple, for of course there are higher stages, higher planes, to which we all hope to aspire, and eventually we shall reach the ultimate when we will be released from the continuous round of karma, which binds us to the earth.

When we have a strong belief, indeed a knowledge, we should not allow anyone to divert us from it, because we have to answer only for ourselves, and another person's ideas and beliefs will not help any of us in the long run. It is no use telling St Peter, 'I took this path because my friend advised it,' for our friend will not be able to help us on the day of reckoning, if indeed he is around, which is unlikely.

Heaven forbid that the above should look like a sermon but I do feel strongly about people allowing themselves to be influenced against their own feelings, when they KNOW they are in the right. Ever since I had an embarrassing experience many years ago I have not allowed myself to follow another person's suggestions when I know my own way is best for me.

I was taking a practical examination with another nurse, and we had to prepare a bed for a certain type of heart patient. It was not just a simple test in a hospital ward but rather in an examination room of the General Nursing Council for England and Wales. The examiner came up by which time my colleague had moved away, and I KNEW the bed was prepared incorrectly. 'Why did you do it that way?' I was asked, and of course I didn't know what to say, but it was a lesson well learned. Since that time I have always had the courage to stand by my convictions.

And then a scholar said, Speak of Talking
And he answered, saying:
You talk when you cease to be at peace
with your thoughts;
And when you can no longer dwell in the
solitude of your heart you live in your
lips, and sound is a diversion and a pastime.

And in much of your talking, thinking is
half murdered.
For thought is a bird of space, that in a
cage of words may indeed unfold its wings
but cannot fly.

The Real us is silent; the acquired is
talkative.

Kahlil Gibran

TEN

With election news everywhere, specifically in Canada and
Great Britain, it seems a suitable moment to enlarge on my
previous statement regarding the politics of Uruguay. The
nine man Council who ran the country was composed of
nine members of the elected party and three members from
the opposing party. The length of parliament was a four-
year tenure, after which further elections would take place.
It was the first four 'runners' who took a one-year term at
the presidency, during the four-year period, and soon after
we left Uruguay the system was changed; the country re-

turned to its former system of a single executive administration, under the Colorados who had been in power for a period of ninety years until their defeat in 1958.

Our sponsors fully expected the Colorados would regain power in nineteen sixty-two but they were disappointed, they had to wait a further four years, when a retired air force general, Oscar Gestido, became president, and he died shortly thereafter.

How did the two parties get their names? Well they are derived from the colours each used in many civil wars for almost a century before it was realized that 'ballots were better than bullets' for deciding political questions. Each of the major parties have within them smaller 'parties' which range from 'leftist' to extreme conservative. Each 'party' has neighbourhood political clubs around which each community's activities are centred. Instead of a four-year term of office, elections are now held every five years.

President Gestido had embarked on an austerity programme, which cut back on welfare and government spending, but his successor, previously Vice-President, although of the same party did not follow strictly in his predecessor's footsteps. The Uruguayan people are not fond of too many controls, and their political history is fascinating.

The time came for us to think of returning to Canada, Mr U was involved in other ventures and we had not seen him for some time, and it seemed we had fulfilled our purpose, and there was no reason for staying longer.

Miss Ku'ei had been sick and the young veterinarian had been called to treat her. After diagnosing an attack of nephritis, and prescribing medication, he left and soon Ku'ei appeared normal again. She had become used to the warmer, more temperate climate, and we hoped she would adjust to the cold and snow back in Canada. However the Guv commented one day, 'You know, it will not be good for Ku'ei. She will not like the change and she may not be with us very long after we return.' I was to learn the truth of those words when Ku'ei departed but there was nothing we could do about it.

It was necessary to contact the Canadian Consulate so that everything would be in order for our return to that country; we had been away for almost two years and were still only Landed Immigrants so it was necessary to obtain official sanction, before making the journey.

Once more we had to make travel plans and that meant an enquiry of the Mormac line regarding a rough time table of cargo ships and available berths. Finally we were informed that they could accommodate us in March, so we made our reservations some weeks ahead, and obtained our tickets right there in the Moore McCormack office, with their representative.

We would have two summers that year, since we would leave in the South American autumn, arriving back to Canada in the spring. That would be nice. The few friends we had made were sorry to see us preparing to leave, and it was hard to explain it was not their country or their city which we found unsatisfactory. In particular I remember a pharmacist who expressed the thought that perhaps we did not find his people good enough to live amongst. The Uruguayans are a very sensitive people, which is part of their charm, especially when they tell you, 'My home is yours.'

We used to visit a bakery whose owners came from Holland, and they talked frequently of Canada and even after we returned they continued to correspond with us with the idea of emigrating here. However, their efforts were not successful, or they changed their minds, and gradually communication ceased.

There was the French lady from Bel Horizon; she had

visited us several times and she promised to keep in touch with us, as did a teacher who was a great fan of Lobsang Rampa; and Alicia, who had helped us with translations and who came to see us infrequently.

During the remaining days we drove around to take a last look at some of the places we had come to know. El Cerro was interesting, the little mountain where lived the poorer people, the paens, the protuberance which inspired the Portuguese sailor to exclaim, 'Monte vide eu' when he realized they were approaching land. Legend has it that Ferdinand Magellan, while sailing around South America to the Philippines, sailed some distance up the Plata river, when a lookout spotted the 'little mountain'.

Ku'ei was always happiest when motoring so we took her for a long drive, along the Rambla, skirting the water, right on past Pocitos beach to Carrasco, returning through the city, passing the big 'Carcel', the prison, where one could see guards patrolling on the roof. The prison was quite near Bel Horizon, as one approached the city.

So our days in Uruguay were drawing to a close, the country which, due to the richness of potash in its soil, has been called 'The Purple Land'.

The grand essentials
to happiness
in this life are
something to do
something to love
and something
to hope for.

Joseph Addison

DOWN TO RIO

On our return voyage the *Mormaclake* took us to Rio – a
place which conjures up so many dream-like fantasies of
fun and merriment. How many of us have thought, with
Rudyard Kipling,

> 'And I'd like to roll to Rio
> Some day before I'm old.'

One of the most beautiful sights of my life was witnessed
in the bay of Rio de Janeiro. It was in the morning, early,
and the Sugar Loaf Mountain rose before us in the early
morning mist. From the top of the mountain, on the peak
which is called the Corcovado, rose the massive Christ-
figure. I have been told that up close the figure is impressive,
and the view from the top is simply indescribable.

The statue, which was inaugurated in 1931 is one hundred
feet in height and weighs seven hundred tons. Designed by
a Frenchman, Paul Landowski, and paid for by contri-
bution of the people of Rio, the head alone weighs thirty
tons, each arm weighs thirty tons, and each hand eight tons.

This edifice must be one of the wonders of the world,

and the travel guides tell us that the best time to visit the statue is in the late afternoon, about one hour before sunset. Fodor's goes on to say, 'The effect of the reddening sun against the buildings and the sea far below will leave you gasping. Then wait patiently and one by one the lights of the town will start to come on, like fireflies awakening for the evening. Within half an hour the city will be dressed in sparkling diamonds and silhouetted against the dark shapes of Sugar Loaf and the blackening waters of the bay and ocean.'

Such sights as this nourish the spirit and the memory lingers for all time. A simpler sight, but no less inspiring, was the early morning gathering of fishing boats in Howth harbour, Ireland, when the sun formed reflections in the water, all peaceful, awaiting the activities of the day.

Brazil is an exciting place, and the Guv says it has a great future, when it will become one of the most evolved countries of the world, doing its part in the evolvement of a greater perfection for mankind. There is a certain gentleman in that country who, perhaps unaware of it himself, is already actually paving the way. He is guiding his country's thinking, through the literature he places before the people.

If I were at the beginning of my life and able to choose the place where I wanted to live, it is not unlikely that I should choose such a country where the people are lively and fun-loving but still of serious thought.

Especially since knowing the Story of Tadalinka, our Autumn lady, I would be interested in knowing more of Brazil.

I love you
the more in that
I believe you have
liked me for
my own sake
and for
nothing else.

John Keats

A BOY FROM BRAZIL

A little boy, aged seven, his little frame shrivelled by leu-kaemia, demanded that doctors let his failing life take its course. He had already taped an articulate message of hope to others facing death.

He asked his mother to remove the oxygen machine that was keeping him alive. 'He said, "Mother, turn off the oxygen, I don't need it anymore,"' commented his Mother. 'I turned it off,' she said. 'Then he held my hand and a big smile came to his face as he said, "It is time." Then he left.'

The boy died at his home after deciding details of his funeral and where he was to be buried. His doctor said the oxygen was not essential to his survival but did provide some comfort during the child's painful last days.

When he was three-and-a-half the boy became associated with a local group who followed the precepts of an ancient religion, and it was his fascination with this philosophy that gave him the belief that death 'was like a passageway, a walk into another galaxy', as he said on his tape.

His message was recorded by a volunteer worker for a

group called Hospice, which works with the dying and their families. When the volunteer asked the boy why he wanted to die, he said: 'Because I am so sick. When you are dead, and a spirit in heaven, you don't have all the aches and pains. And sometimes, if you want to, you can visit this life but you can't come back into your own life.

'If you don't hang on to your body and let yourself ease away,' he said on the tape, 'it is not so painful.'

If you love something,
set it free,
If it comes back,
It is yours,
If it doesn't,
It never was.

ELEVEN

As the *Mormaclake* steamed along the Atlantic towards the United States, one was provided with good opportunities for reflection; just to relax on the deck with no interruptions or disturbances of any sort was good for the body and refreshing for the mind.

I found myself contemplating the life we had but recently left, admiring the leaders whose vision had resulted in making Uruguay one of the most literate countries of South America. There are those who believe that compulsory state education is wrong and that you should receive an education only if you are able to pay for it. Perhaps those people are right but from the point of view of one who benefited from the system, I can only applaud it.

In many ways children are victims of the society in which they are born; when faced with family opposition, and without the aid of the State, they would, in many cases, succumb to the position of unpaid child labour.

Being brought up in a community in which physical survival was the main concern I could identify with Mark Twain when he said, 'I wanted schooling more than I was able to get. I had a parent who considered if a boy could plough a straight furrow – and a girl could make butter and bake bread, that was a whole lot more use in the world!!!' I like the further statement of this man who realized that 'book learning' was not the only important thing in life. He said, 'I never let schooling interfere with my education.'

At school I must have been looked upon as something of a freak for, strangely enough, I liked to study. Fortunately children do not *always* see how they appear to others, so they go ahead and do what they want to do, and I did have the satisfaction of hearing my teacher tell me, as I went out into the world, 'Well, you are one of the few of my students who are doing something with their life.' That was a REAL compliment, I felt.

Thus the days passed, and the strolls on deck, watching the moon and the stars, or asleep in the stateroom, proved to be a healthy and satisfying experience. The return journey had been rather less sad, for we had adjusted to the loss of our Fifi, the loss which had clouded the outward voyage.

Our first port of call, the Captain told us, would be Jacksonville, Florida, so, as I had never set foot in that State, I felt somewhat excited about it. We had been told, also, that passengers are expected to disembark at the first stop but, since the ship's radio was not functioning, making it impossible to contact Head Office, the Captain agreed we would be allowed to stay aboard until the freighter reached New York. Of course this was wonderful news to us because it was simply a matter of catching a train from New York to Canada, whereas it would be a much greater problem to make one's way from Florida.

Miss Ku'ei was most concerned, knowing a cat was not so easily accepted, travelwise, as a human animal, although the US railroads *will* accept cats, travelling in ordinary passenger cars, which alas they will not allow in Canada. For once a 'malfunction' or a 'non-function' instrument was acceptable.

It had been necessary to supply a United States address to the authorities, though I cannot understand why, since we were only in transit, merely passing through; however rules are rules, even if some people say they were made to be broken, so we offered the name and address of a friend who lived in Michigan, expecting to arrive at Detroit, and then to Windsor.

As things turned out we found it more convenient to re-enter Canada via Buffalo and on to Fort Erie, where reservations had been made at the Fort Erie Hotel.

A few weeks later our Michigan friend was contacted by the authorities to see whether we were still in the country – Sometimes I wonder at the ease with which criminals and other unauthorized persons can take up residence in America when honest citizens are so well supervised.

Cats have very sad faces. They look at
you a long time and think about you. They
are peaceful to have around.

A school-child

TWELVE

It was a nice feeling, for me, to be back in Canada where I
was familiar with the language and the customs, and it was
April, which is one of the nicest times of the year.

Fort Erie Hotel was very comfortable and the owner,
who lived nearby, gave instructions that we were to be
given every attention so that our stay would be pleasant.

At that time accommodation was hard to come by, unlike the city where I now live – so much demolition and
building goes on here that if you didn't look out of the
window every day you might not recognize your surroundings. Calgary, the city of the future, it is called.

Since there were a number of factories in the area, the
available living space was always well-filled with the
workers and their families. The two small apartment buildings hardly ever had any vacancies, so it was necessary for
us to comb the newspaper advertisements very carefully,
together with making all verbal enquiries possible, hoping
to find something suitable.

Eventually we were offered a small flat, situated over a
garage or similar, the ground floor having been used as a
storage place, even as an office, when we rented the upper
part. It was convenient for shopping, being on the opposite
side of Jarvis to where we had lived before our trip to South
America, and the front window looked out towards the

railway station. The landlord lived in the adjoining house though it made no difference to us, for hardly ever did we see either him or his wife. Sometimes, you know, landlords look at tenants as 'something the cat brought in'.

Having always been of a lethargic type, I find Canada invigorating, except for coastal areas. During our stay in New Brunswick, at Saint John, I used to feel tired, likewise Vancouver, which I found anything but beneficial. The sea is considered relaxing, but if one has trouble in staying conscious that seems to be overdoing things; mountains I enjoy and I have felt more energetic since living in Calgary than at almost any time of my adult life. Yes, I must have been awfully dopey before – but it's nice to be fairly alert now, though I still have a long way to go!!

It has been said that if one is in the right environment it can make a big difference to one's physical health, and mental condition; certain individuals need one thing and others something else. There must be something in the belief that it is helpful for a person to locate somewhere which is similar to their birthplace. Of course a theory cannot be proven by one case alone but I find it interesting that I was born and brought up among the hills in the 'high country', not unlike my present environment.

It is necessary to get one's feet in contact with the ground whenever possible, and those who are able to step out of their own front door into their gardens are very fortunate, while apartment dwellers are at a disadvantage. Being able to live and work close to the soil enables one to tune in to the natural earth currents, thus country dwellers, especially those who work on the land, are amongst the most healthy and happy of the population.

Miss Ku'ei and I spent a pleasant summer together; as I have written elsewhere we used to take a little walk every day, after lunch, sometimes across to the little railroad station, and sit in the waiting room awhile because Ku'ei, like all Siamese Cat persons, was very inquisitive and she enjoyed watching human activities.

At other times we lingered by the side of the road, Ku'ei in harness and leash so she would not suddenly 'take off', for Siamese cats are perhaps a little more unpredictable than most types. She had become so used to wearing her harness, even when out driving, that she refused to go outside without it. It represented security and she looked upon it as her outdoor dress.

Gladys, too, became a frequent visitor once more, and we spent interesting moments discussing our various experiences of the previous two years, although we had all corresponded during that time. Being interested in all artistic and intellectual pursuits Gladys enjoyed hearing of the progress made by Uruguay in this direction. Having heard of the famous Gaucho sculpture she wanted to know if it was 'as good' as it had been painted; we assured her that indeed it was, one of the two best examples of Uruguayan sculpture; the gaucho on his horse, by Zorilla de San Martin, cast in bronze and depicting the courage and freedom of the gaucho.

We talked of the other example of Uruguayan sculpture which is known far and wide and which is situated in the Parque José Batille y Ordoñez, another bronze statue, by Belloni. This is a life-size statue depicting six oxen hauling a covered wagon and a gaucho directing the oxen. The statue is known as the covered wagon.

We all enjoyed the afternoons with our friend and she would stay to have tea with us, telling of events in Canada while we had been away. During the earlier days, at Cedar House, Gladys used to speak of a young lawyer in Niagara Falls and how everyone predicted a rosy future for her in politics, so we were interested to know this lady politician was still showing promise, in the Federal field.

Now no longer in the government, Miss La Marsh is still very much in the public eye as the author of two books. I appreciated her recent comment, when she was interviewed. 'Anyway I have beaten that one-book thing.' It was her answer to those who had said she would not produce anything more. Not the first time that someone has been criticized for failing to follow up a first book with another.

On the other hand, who needs to put out anything more if they are Richard Adams, the British author, who wrote *Watership Down*, that beautiful story set in the English country-side, which was later made into a successful film?

Then there was our friend from Michigan who came to see us: we would walk down to the Parkway by the Niagara River, filling in with news we had missed in our absence. Valeria was extremely pleased at our return for she had been a fairly frequent guest in the previous years, and she had taken a trip to Montevideo while we were in that city. She had arrived armed with a Spanish/English dictionary and, being well prepared as always, her Spanish vocabulary was more than adequate. One might well envy Valeria for her alert mental abilities.

In this work, when it should be found that much
is omitted,
let it not be forgotten that much likewise
is performed.

Dr. Samuel Johnson,
in the Preface of his Dictionary
of the English Language

THIRTEEN

There was little to disturb the even tempo of life during
that summer; it was just as well because the situation would
change the following year when we were to experience
plenty of activity. That is one nice thing about life, one has
quiet spells which allow for thought, and then comes a
spurt of activity which makes for variety, adding a spice to
living.

A few weeks after we returned to Canada there came a
letter from Montevideo, and we wondered about the contents, who could have sent the missile since the handwriting
seemed unfamiliar. We need not have felt concern for it
was a pleasant letter, written by the mother of the 'young-
man-landlord' of our apartment of Calle Constituente. This
lady merely wanted to express her relief and mild astonishment at the meticulous condition in which she found the
premises when she called to check things after our departure. Oh, yes, we had excelled ourselves, leaving the
carpets and rugs freshly shampooed and the property all
ready for the next tenant.

Further Madame (she was French, remember) Landlord
advised us that anytime we wished to visit Uruguay in the

future she would be happy to accommodate us. 'I have a nice apartment at Punta del Este,' she wrote, 'and please do let me know when you expect to come.' She assumed there was no question as to IF we were coming – only when?

I feel somewhat in the position of an expert regarding rented accommodation, and I have to admit that some people treat another person's property in a terrible manner; yet an owner can be very unpleasant sometimes, making things difficult for the lessee. Once, in one of the less desirable areas of London an old lady confronted us with the remark, 'You didn't chop up the wardrobe, I hope.' Apparently she had known people damage her furniture but to us it came as something of a shock to be thus confronted.

So the days passed, pleasantly, but something seemed to warn me that possibly this could be the last summer we would have the company of our Miss Ku'ei, who had experienced much of life's hardships, so we tried to give her as much pleasure as possible. Pleasure to Ku'ei meant riding in an automobile, so this we did about twice every week. In the evenings she and I would watch selected television programmes, and this she enjoyed too, especially variety shows and programmes such as *What's My Line*, something which originated in England. We liked Dean Martin, a nice simple show, but now Dean has changed his style, his appearance, and his way of life, so I have switched to another programme.

Perhaps I should point out that this is not a TV oriented household, nor has it ever been; in the early days of our Canadian life we had one for awhile, but in those days the quality was not so good as now. The Guv used to explain there were not so many 'lines' to the inch resulting in a more crude picture, and he saw 'between the lines' therefore there was no enjoyment for him, but to someone such as myself it seemed to make little difference.

So we disposed of our instrument and did without for several years. However, Mama San, who likes to keep a finger on the pulse of things; and not being clairvoyant, or believing everything printed in magazines or newspapers (knowing from experience that much of what is printed is biased, if not actually untrue) likes to form her own opinions on world affairs, and people. For that reason a small portable television is useful.

Unlike Miss Ku'ei, Cleo and Taddy never took to the 'tube' but instead they have been known to show extreme displeasure that anyone should waste their time over such nonsense. Still, taken in moderation it can be quite relaxing; just yesterday evening it was quite entertaining when, amongst the celebrities, one saw on the screen a well-known British novelist who is at present visiting the United States. A lady who has had published over a hundred novels. I had not seen even a picture of her since my days in England, yet there she was wearing a dazzling gown created, as she said, 'By the Queen's dressmaker'.

As I watched my programme from Las Vegas Miss Cleo sat in the hallway, within sight, viewing me with an utterly disapproving air.

Wherever we have lived we continued to have a keen interest in photography and Fort Erie was no exception. Although I had done most of my picture-taking in Ireland, amidst the lovely scenery, the Guv had continued to regale us with his camera magic; the most commonplace subjects glowed with life.

I was not surprised, then, when a few weeks following our return to Canada he announced he wanted to try out a polaroid and perhaps he could take a few shots of me.

So I sat in the living room of our Courtright Street apartment, my chair set apart from the window so that the light fell on my features, idly day-dreaming, while preparations were made and the camera ready. 'Smile now,' said the Guv, so I did, whimsically, as he touched the shutter and began to time the processing.

Colour film is slightly slower than monochrome but soon the picture was released and an image began to appear. In those days one stood with a watch, timing the process; release the print too soon and the result was too faint – too long and it was over-exposed – but now everything is automatic so there is no necessity for that sort of timing.

Well, the resulting portrait was quite acceptable, even to me, since, like most people, I have never been easy to satisfy as far as taking my photograph was concerned, so I expressed my appreciation, but that was not the end of the experiment.

As we chatted I noticed the Guv still held the camera in the same position and in the direction I had been sitting, and when he pressed the release I wondered what he was up to, just pointing the camera towards the bare wall. In a short time I saw what he had done and I marvelled, for there was another print, exactly like the first, except it was slightly paler in colour.

'What is that,' I asked. 'Magic?'

So he explained that the 'impression' had lingered for the time it took to make a second picture and the Guv, being able to see this, decided to capture it. Possibly some people will find it hard to accept but, believe it or not, it is true enough; it really was the way I have described.

To anyone who might suggest the picture had been copied I would say that was not possible because the Polaroid, as it then was, was not capable of copying; to copy one needs a special attachment which we did not have. To the Guv, none of this is strange, he often says that the camera sees much more than the human eye and this I know for on seeing a picture of something familiar, a scene outside, or in a room, one has heard the remark, 'You know, in all the times I have looked at that, there is something I never noticed.' But what I have just described *is* a rather different matter.

Fame is the scentless sunflower,
    with gaudy crown of gold,
But friendship is the breathing rose
    with sweets in every fold,

Oliver Wendell Holmes

FOURTEEN

In the summer months, especially, Fort Erie is a busy place; just across the Peace Bridge from Buffalo this entrance to Canada is used by many United States citizens who own, or rent, cottages in a vacation area known as Crystal Beach, near Ridgeway, just a few miles from the border. The shores of Lake Erie, the fourth largest of the Great Lakes and the most southerly, are ideal in summer; the dwellings are almost on the edge of the water, so there is a constant stream of automobiles passing through Fort Erie right through the summer season, mostly headed for Crystal Beach.

One day there came a knock on our door and I went down the stairs to the front entrance (not that there was any other) to see what was happening, because we had very few callers and mainly by previous arrangement. Here I found a man we knew, and he held in his arms a little cat, or more accurately, a kitten, and he handed the creature to me. The man knew of our interest in cats so, apparently, he had figured he would not be unwelcome if he came to us with his problem.

'What's this?' I asked. 'What do you want me to do with your cat, or isn't it yours?'

My thoughts were racing as he talked. Such a pretty little

bundle of grey fur, I was thinking, and would I be able to adopt it?

'Well, Ma'am,' continued the man. 'Just a few minutes ago, along the road, there, a car stopped, slowed down and something was thrown out, then off went the driver at high speed.' He continued, 'I went over to see what it was and, blow me, I found the cat.'

Looking a bit self-conscious and appealing he said, 'Can you take it, please?' What could I do? Hurrying up the stairs I quickly told the Guv and he agreed I should bring the little cat-person in, so I told the man and he expressed his appreciation, and hurried off.

First of all the kitten must have food, she certainly appeared very hungry, because you must always see to their needs such as food, and elimination, after selecting a quiet spot, preferably a separate room, where the cat-person will not be disturbed.

When I stipulate a separate room, it is assumed you already have a pet, as I had, so that the newcomer can feed, rest and become oriented without interruption. Haven't you noticed that, without any disturbing factor, a cat while eating his supper will frequently stop, look around for danger, then resume his meal? Instinct, no doubt, a racial memory, carried from pre-domestic times.

The little grey kitten soon felt at home, her purring was just like a kettle on the boil, and I began to wonder whether she would be able to stay with us, permanently. Her only problem seemed to be a weakness in her legs, probably caused through malnutrition and possible injury as she hit the ground, after being tossed out of the actually moving car.

A further discussion was called for, this time Miss Ku'ei had a word or two to say – and her remarks were most tolerant, not having come face to face with the possible rival she could afford to be magnanimous.

But after much thought, a consultation with a veterinarian, and the opinion that our future was not sufficiently settled to contemplate adopting another cat, it was found necessary to let the little person pursue another path.

The S.P.C.A. was contacted and one of the officials, who lived in the town and who was off duty, asked me to take the little cat around to her house which I did that same evening. On the way I called upon a family, the mother having shown interest, so they could see the little Grey and decide if they wanted to take her; when I arrived the mother and her daughters were waiting but they could not decide among themselves so we left, the little cat and I, continuing our unhappy walk.

As I reached the house of the S.P.C.A. official, she answered our knock, reaching out to take the kitten, and tossing her into the bathroom, on her way to the living room, where I had to sit down and provide details as to how the cat had come into my 'possession' etcetera.

In the living room I noticed a mature tom cat whose age, the mistress said, was nearing twenty-one years; a cat who needed constant attention, including frequent cat-doctor visits to maintain his conditions. I like to think the elderly cat was the reason for little Grey having to be in the bathroom; when you have reached your sunset years you cannot stand children of any species upsetting your status quo. But my heart went out to the kitten!

So, after signing the papers the official had presented, including address and a few more details, I said goodbye to the little person and left, concluding one of the most unhappy missions I have ever undertaken. Since that time I have thought that it would be wiser to take a 'stray' or an abandoned pet straight to the cat hospital and arrange to have it sent Home while one waited, so that it could start life again under happier conditions, not as an UNWANTED of the world.

Was it fate, coincidence, or what, which brought that creature into our lives? A creature resembling in so many ways Blue Grey who we had known while in Montevideo, and who, in the not-so-distant future, we would know again – our autumn lady.

> I don't mind dying but I would prefer
> not to be around when it happens.
>
> *Woody Allen*

FIFTEEN

Sometimes a doomed nature animal performs a service for a human animal which results in a reprieve, a reversal of the death sentence, and this was what happened in the case of Zorba, the dog owned by a Greek fisherman.

Zorba was sentenced to die because it was said he was a pest; the neighbours of Christos Spyrakis, the fisherman, in the tiny village of Hierapetra on Crete, had begun to complain about the black and white mongrel. 'The dog used to howl and bark sometimes at night,' admitted the owner. 'He would also chase a chicken or a cat, like any dog would, but this was only playful, and he never went for a kill or anything vicious.'

Nevertheless, neighbours demanded he get rid of Zorba – and the local police told him either to give the dog away or have him 'destroyed'. Nobody wanted Zorba, so Spyrakis took the only course open to him. Early one morning he set out in his boat with the dog and a sack of stones, to use as weights, to send his faithful companion to the bottom of the Mediterranean Sea. The trip would end eight years of devotion, from the time he first found the abandoned newborn pup and saved his life.

Miles out at sea Spyrakis realized that while he'd been lost in his sad thoughts, a storm had come up; the fishing boat, *Zorba 2*, was in trouble. A freak wave smashed into the boat, overturning it and sending Spyrakis and the dog, Zorba, into the sea.

After half an hour of battling the fierce waves, the fisherman felt himself giving in. 'I was exhausted and swallowing water,' he said. Occasionally I caught glimpses of Zorba, but it was hopeless to try and keep together. 'Then, in semiconsciousness, I realized that Zorba was tugging at the collar of my jacket. To tell the truth, I didn't think it was much help at the time, that it was all useless anyway –'

But somehow Zorba managed to pull his master miles to shore, then run to Crete's Coastal Highway where his frantic barking stopped a car. The courageous dog led the three motorists to his master, lying face down at the water's edge. While the rugged fisherman, nearly drowned and badly bruised, spent a week recovering in the hospital – the same neighbours, who had requested that Zorba be killed, fed the devoted dog. 'It was those same neighbours who asked me to spare the dog's life,' said Police Captain Nikos Alexakis. 'It was much more pleasant to decide on sparing the dog's life, and rewarding the dog, rather than being made to ratify the death warrant.' When Spyrakis left the hospital, Alexakis was waiting for him in the hospital lobby.

'Your dog will not die,' he told the fisherman. 'He's a hero now for saving your life, and all your neighbours have decided that they want him to stay.' For his heroic feat, Zorba was awarded the equivalent of a St Nicholas Cross, given for bravery at sea in saving the lives of others.

'I may have lost *Zorba* the boat – but I can get another boat anytime,' said Spyrakis. 'But I only have one Zorba the dog – and he is irreplaceable!'

This story came to me as I was writing the previous chapter and it seemed fitting to include it here.

One aspect of the account I found disturbing, and rather puzzling. Why should anyone take a creature away out to sea and try to drown it, when a veterinarian could perform euthanasia so simply, quickly and without pain? Perhaps most people are unaware of the shock and delay caused in

77

the process of drowning and, in the case of the fisherman, he may not have had easy access to a pet hospital even if he could afford it.

As a child I have known of people drowning unwanted kittens but this method of disposing of little 'pets' is considered painful and a lingering, drawn out, process. Would anyone drown a baby? Or throw an infant out of a car? Not unless they were mentally disturbed! So why treat a pet differently.

Lobsang Rampa has quite frequently made the remark that humans in general tend to underestimate the mentality of animal animals, and that we would be surprised if we could understand their mental processes, that of cats in particular.

It is not beyond reason to accept the fact that the cat fraternity knew that there was a possible vacancy in the Rampa household – we had gone away with two cats and returned with only one, so why not arrange for a replacement? I have been in the fortunate position of receiving messages from these people, via interpretation by the Guv, so to me it is very real.

I know some people consider it a crazy idea but, as I quoted in the front of my book *Tigerlily*, according to our own Shakespeare, 'There are more things in heaven and earth than ye wot of.' If, instead of keeping our noses to the ground, we were to look up and around us, and LISTEN instead of making noises, we might be startled to find how much our awareness had increased.

It's nice for children to have pets
Until the pets start having children.

SIXTEEN

That last Fort Erie summer was a time for remembering and pondering – such times are very useful and necessary in everyone's lives.

It was from the window of our Courtwright Street apartment that I had the interesting experience of seeing an unidentified flying object, through a powerful telescope. The Guv has written about the incident, how he called 'Mrs Old Man' to come and witness the, at that time, somewhat rare sight. An experience to dwell in the mind forever, this huge object, with its myriad, swirling colours.

We spent many leisure moments listening to music on tapes and records, and Miss Ku'ei loved to get settled in her own chair and enjoy the rousing Irish songs, and lullabies. It is quite disturbing when you are having a quiet musical moment and someone rushes into the room, breaking the spell. That is one of my memories and *I* was the culprit, having been out shopping, and not realizing until too late that I had broken the peacefulness for the Guv and Ku'ei; my remorse and apologies did not help the situation very much.

It was a time when we had many interesting conversations, listening to stories of the Guv's homeland, and marvelling at the different way of life, its customs and the depth of spirituality among the devoted lamas.

We talked of our days in England, and I mentioned an experience which took place at a London main line railway station, in the early years of our life together. We were living in a southwest suburb of London and the Guv had been away from home for a few days; he was due to return that evening and I was to go along to meet that particular train.

It was a summer evening, still clear in my memory, and I prepared myself leisurely, filling in the moments by playing with Mr T. Catt – the hero of *Tigerlily*, who was our guardian in those days. Eventually it was time to leave so, with a hug and a pat, I left T. Catt in charge, and went off on my rendezvous with the Guv. I felt, on that evening, that the 'spheres' were very close together, which gave me a feeling of peace and, I suppose, heightened my vibrations (a much maligned word these days).

There have been other times, usually around twilight that I have felt the same and made the comment, 'Just now heaven and earth appear very close together,' and it is, invariably, accompanied by a particularly uplifting feeling. Well, having completed my journey through the London traffic, I entered the railway station, and was allowed on to the platform where the train was just pulling slowly in, and gradually it came to a complete stop. In those days it was quite exciting to make a journey by train, or to go and meet someone who had so travelled; air travel is sensational in comparison, but you cannot compare an airport lounge with an old-fashioned railway station, for romance.

So the train having stopped, the guard unlocked the doors and steps were placed in position, for the convenience of passengers who were preparing to alight. Suddenly a sea of people approached and passed me as I stood there, and I began to think the Guv had missed his train.

Then, all at once a voice addressed me, 'Hello, Ra'ab, didn't you see me?'

'How could I see you?' I answered, 'in this brilliant light?'

In my confusion I rationalized it was the sunlight which had almost blinded me, except that it was sundown, and the station was completely covered in, not open to the sky. And then I saw the Guv, smiling down upon me. 'Come along, let us get home,' he said. So away we went.

Being ignorant I did not then know that *anything*, a person or an object, may vibrate so rapidly that it appears as pure light to an onlooker. So that was the kind of thing we discussed, and the Guv pointed out how two people may be watching the sky on the appearance of a so called flying saucer, for instance; one person may be able to see the craft while the other standing near may see nothing – only one of them being on a 'harmonic' – but that is not a valid reason for denying their existence.

One has heard of certain individuals, especially in the Far East, who are able to make themselves invisible to others, and I have often wondered about it – it must come about through a special method of breathing which causes the person to vibrate so rapidly that the image is beyond the range of the average human, but possibly visible to a clairvoyant. It would be quite a strange experience to be spoken to by an apparently disembodied voice. Enough to make one jump, don't you think? Still if we just stop and consider – it is on something the same lines as the high-pitched whine of a dog, about which everyone is familiar, a sound which again, cannot be registered by the average human hearing process. Phenomena such as this I find absolutely fascinating; really, many things which come under the heading 'occult' have a very simple explanation if one takes the trouble to find out, instead of dubbing everything not understood as mysterious or unorthodox.

I would rather have written those lines
(*Gray's Elegy*) than take Quebec.

James Wolfe
on the night before the
storming of Quebec.

SEVENTEEN

So the weeks passed until it was autumn, then came the
cold of November, with the prospect of a winter in the
snow belt of the Niagara escarpment. Quite a change after
two years in the South American sun.

Our 'flat' above a garage space was not completely winter-
ized so we viewed its approach with less than enthusiasm,
wondering how we would survive, literally.

With the passing of summer and early fall warmth, Miss
Ku'ei suffered just as the Guv had predicted, but what could
we do except try to keep her warm and comfortable. It is
well known that anyone who has a kidney problem, whether
human or 'animal', finds their discomfort lessened when
their body is warm, together with their surroundings. Ku'ei
suffered a recurrence of the cystitis which had troubled her
before, and for a time she kept awakening me every morning around four o'clock, crying out and telling me of her
discomfort, and she would just wander around the place.

You know that expression, 'Tugging at your heart-
strings!' Well, without appearing sloppy I would say that
is what it did to me, hearing my little cat in pain, and so
little I could do. We had no telephone so, early as I dared
to disturb our local veterinarian, I would go down the stairs
to the public phone, just by our entrance, to ask his advice.

Dr Reid was always helpful, and sympathetic; he would suggest continuing with the pills he had previously prescribed, asking that Ku'ei be kept warm and given sufficient water to drink.

To us and our cat-children, Dr Reid has always shown the greatest consideration and, apart from his professional services, we developed a friendship with him, and with his kind, efficient wife.

Fortunately we had an electric blanket on our bed so Ku'ei would dive under the covers; in a short time she had manufactured sufficient heat to alleviate her renal discomfort. In the daytime a hot water bottle would serve the same purpose when tucked under the blanket on her chair.

By the time Christmas came winter really was upon us, and I remember visiting Dr Reid's office on Christmas morning – that's how dedicated he was, having suggested I went along so that he might check over her condition and give Ku'ei a 'booster shot' to aid her appetite, which had suffered too. We would then adjourn to the private quarters of the Reid Family, as on other visits, when Mrs Reid would offer us (me – not Ku'ei) coffee and Christmas cake.

Yes, veterinarians are amongst my closest friends, their wives also. On behalf of so called dumb animals, I would salute them all.

As the new year approached the worst of winter was still to come, as is usual in Canada and particularly so in Ontario. As the snow came we found it falling on the stairs leading up to our flat, in spite of being covered in, and the suite itself was extremely cold. Many were the hours spent in wondering what to do – how to find a warmer place, in a town where there was little to offer. The humans in the family were not finding conditions too bad but you can't put clothes on a little cat, or shoes; Ku'ei was most unwell and unhappy.

So one day, while investigating the Jarvis Street area, which was quite near, being merely one street away, I found myself in the Salvation Army Thrift Shop to enquire about a sign in the window, advertising a flat for rent.

'Oh,' said the man behind the counter, 'that has been vacant for some time. It needed a little attention and immediately the sign went up a man came and rented the flat.' He saw I was looking very disappointed so he volunteered further information. 'The tenant has not yet moved in and truth to tell he didn't appear all that interested – in fact he seemed somewhat half-hearted about the whole deal.'

The Thrift Shop man offered to give me the name of the half-hearted tenant, and the address, suggesting I go along and discuss the matter because, anyway, it seemed a lot of space for one man who lived alone, and who already had comfortable rooms which seemed to be satisfactory for his needs. 'You'd better take a look at the premises first,' said the Thrift Shop man. 'It's possible you won't find it suitable, so it's much better to look first.' Not strictly ethical, I thought, but it must be all right to look, so I did, and it seemed to be quite suitable for our needs. Since there was no alternative I couldn't do other than give it serious consideration; the worst feature was the peculiar stuffy atmosphere, especially in the large room.

It was a bitterly cold day, snowing, and I felt rather weary as I made my way to see the other man who was, fortunately, quite amiable. As the Thrift Shop man had said the tenant seemed almost anxious to cancel his contract, for a small consideration, so I hurried home with the news thinking 'anything is worth a try and you might be lucky.' I visualized Miss Ku'ei making a quick recovery, soon to be quite well again, in the new warm surroundings. My hopes were short-lived however; it was other influences which dashed them – the ever present negative forces of the world.

> Anyone can sympathize with the sufferings of a
> friend, but it requires a very fine nature to
> sympathize with a friend's success.
>
> *Oscar Wilde*

GOODBYE MISS KU'EI

Even as we prepared to move to our new home trouble
descended upon our household in the form of the media,
and this episode has been recorded in one of my previous
books, *Pussywillow*.

A boy in England took his own life while experimenting
with electricity, and it was widely reported that he had one
of Lobsang Rampa's books in his possession. It didn't matter that he would have had various other books in his room
by other authors – an item involving a well-known author
would make the best copy.

First a reporter from the local weekly came to us, then
another newsman from Toronto, who made a second visit to
clarify something he had missed the first time. The second
time he was accompanied by a newswoman and all the time
Miss Ku'ei looked on, sadly.

We had suffered greatly through the media, all due to
the jealousy and spite of a small group of individuals from
England and Europe, and the Guv told me that Miss Ku'ei
was thinking, 'What, again! Will they never allow us to
live our lives in peace?' She thought, 'What's the use?'

Having made the commitment, and having advised the
present landlord of our intention to terminate the contract,
in a short time we were installed in the new premises.

Ku'ei and I were allotted the long bedroom and we never

did get rid of that strange odour, which reminded us of something not very pleasant, in view of our recent experience. Why was there such an impression of newsprint, printers' ink, around the place, we wondered! Eventually it came to our knowledge that some time previously the place had belonged to a newspaper proprietor, and we were told that it is a devilish thing to get rid of newsprint odour. I believe the room we used must have been where bundles of newspapers were stored.

I continued taking Ku'ei for her once, or twice, weekly drives, and she showed some slight improvement as spring was approaching; we would call upon Dr and Mrs Reid occasionally, and she liked the change of scenery. However, as I have written previously, she eventually succumbed to the physical and nervous strain, and she left us early in March, unfortunately fulfilling the forecast made by the Guv. We had been in Canada less than a year. It was a terribly sad time and I said, 'No more cat-people for me, it is too heart-breaking when they leave.' But that was not to be either.

Father Abbot, I am come to lay my weary
bones among you.

Cardinal Wolsey –
to the Abbot of Leicester Abbey
in November, 1529.

EIGHTEEN

After many years of her companionship it seemed quite
strange to be without a furry feline – and lonesome.

I sat on my bed in the long room, which was also the
large one; I saw the little hassock which had been used by
Ku'ei since the move from Courtwright Street; it had been
purchased especially for her, and for a time, she had been
interested in using the little seat; she had shown a little more
interest in life.

As the days passed I thought very seriously about the
problem of whether I would take on the responsibility of
another cat-person. For one thing I wondered if my own
life would outlast that of another creature; I wouldn't want
to leave my cat to someone else after having spent a number
of years with me, having come to accept my ways and the
ways of my household.

Some people might think my views on the subject rather
strange, but we are all entitled to our views, mine were the
same as those of the Guv, who suggested if I did make a
further commitment I would have to make out a written
statement to the effect that were my life to end first the
veterinarian of the moment would be informed, and he

would undertake to have the cat sent Home, with the least pain and discomfort, in the most humane manner, which is considered to be by injection.

Just recently I was reading a book by Frank MacShane on the life of the author and playwright, Raymond Chandler, who had a beautiful black cat named Taki living with him, and whose picture is included in the book. Now Raymond Chandler is quoted as saying he didn't understand people who hesitated about having a pet in case the pet survived them; he thought that a crazy outlook. Well, I am not so sure about other pets, although dogs have been known to pine on the death of 'master' or 'mistress', but I do know about cats. Even if it did not give up, and just die, a cat who is treated as a person and an equal, will suffer greatly if left on his own, even with other people than his original 'owner'. Even a bird has been known to succumb on losing its owner so how do we know that all creatures are not so affected?

We had heard of a private cattery in Niagara Falls so we telephoned Mrs Later, who operated the little 'cat farm' as a side-line to her main job as a laboratory technician. On hearing of our needs regarding a Siamese cat she said, 'That is no problem'. She had a litter of seal points, about five in all, aged about six weeks, and in another two weeks she would allow them to leave their mother and proceed to new homes.

'Just a minute,' said Mrs Later, as I was about to put down the receiver after arranging to go and see the family that very Saturday evening, 'One little kitty in this litter is a bluish grey colour; don't ask me why because the mother and father are both seal points.'

'Thank you,' I answered. 'I will tell my husband all this and I will come along to your house as soon as possible.'

So I conveyed the message and immediately the Guv

89

said, 'Ra'ab, we *must* have the *blue* kitten.' That will
be the one to replace Miss Ku'ei, and how about arranging
for us to have a companion for her?' Mrs Later had mentioned she was a queen, and not a tom cat.

'Wonderful,' I answered, 'but how will I know which
seal point to choose?'

'Don't be silly,' he continued, 'with all your experience
don't tell me you can't choose a cat!'

What an exciting evening, especially as I was doing something Miss Ku'ei thoroughly approved of, and when I
arrived at the door Mrs Later's children heard the car as
they rushed to let me in.

A lovely log fire in the living room and a bevy of happy
cats and kittens – and Mrs Later 'in her element' with her
lovely family of felines.

'This is Shari, the mother,' she told me, so I greeted Shari
in the proper manner, telling her I would take great care of
her children. Part of the conversation was by telepathy, of
course, for who ever heard of a cat talking to a human? Anyhow, Shari seemed to understand so I turned to her babies.

Apart from the little blue one, there were four more,
completing the family of quintuplets; two little tom kittens
and two queens, all seal points.

'Ah, there you are,' I called to the blue one, smallest of
them all. 'Come, talk to me,' I indicated; as she came towards me, I saw she was a beautiful little cat, very small,
and friendly.

'So that is settled,' I told Mrs Later; 'we will have this
unique creature, a blue grey kitten from a litter of what
should be *all* seal points.'

'How do I choose another,' I thought and Mrs Later
seemed to understand. I had noticed one kitten sitting by
itself, slightly away from the others, and looking very dignified.

'Well, you see this baby,' pointing to the somewhat aloof one, 'she has almost perfect markings so if no one takes her, I plan to keep her here for breeding purposes.' But she intimated she would be happy to have the little person enter the household of Lobsang Rampa. 'Her registration papers carry the name of Cleopatra,' continued Mrs Later, 'and I will feel honoured if you care to continue using it.'

Considering my Egyptian leanings it was no trouble to concur – indeed it was a pleasure – so Cleopatra she has always been, still is, and always will be.

The little blue cat, who became our autumn lady, had been given a temporary exotic name on her papers, with the idea that, if it was unacceptable to the future owner, they could change it, which we did.

She was smaller than Cleopatra, with a short, insignificant tail which eventually became a thing of beauty, with its concentric rings in a darker shade. As I have stated elsewhere, in *Pussywillow*, the Guv decided she resembled a tadpole in comparative size so he began to call her Tad; it seemed insignificant beside her sister's queenly name, however, so she became Miss Tadalinka, a title of which she became justly proud. Their names were of equal length so in that respect they were equal. Who would have thought, at that time, that she would soon become our big Fat Taddy?

Incidentally I might mention that Egypt has had no less than seven queens who bore the name Cleopatra. Perhaps that is the reason so many people claim to have been one of them in a previous life. They couldn't all have been Caesar's Cleo, or Antony's.

SOMEONE –
to talk with
to dance with
to sing with
to eat with
to laugh with
to cry with
to think with
to understand
SOMEONE –
to be my friend

Susan Polis Schultz

NINETEEN

So one Sunday morning, late in March, the ladies Cleopatra and Tadalinka made the first of their car rides, from
Niagara Falls to Fort Erie, a distance of around a score
miles. Having no car then or since, we have had to rely on
the services of taxis and this way our experiences have been
broader, and we have come to know personally a few interesting drivers.

The special driver of the moment, whose lives we place
in his hands each time we venture out, for we are often told
that here in Calgary are the most careless drivers in the
country, if not in the whole North American continent, has
for the past five years made life pleasant for me and for my
felines. As I have documented previously Keith always
anticipates our needs, he takes us right to the places we
want, with no detours, no arguments or anything. Being a
Taurean, let us say that, typically, he prefers to take the
easy way of a peaceful Venusian.

Of course all the drivers are considerate, including ladies such as Jean and Ann, and I mention them here because I believe taxi drivers have quite a difficult life; even here in Calgary at least two have lost their lives recently, at the hands of the public, one young woman being brutally murdered near Banff, after accepting a fare from Calgary. The crime was not committed for merely monetary reasons either; although the taxi was quickly located it was some days before the victim's body was recovered.

When I arrived home with the two kittens, one bluish coloured and the other the colour of a seal the Guv exclaimed, 'Whatever have you brought us?' He thought they were too tiny; not very strong on their feet, and he said, 'Now you have set yourself a job, to make these little people strong and healthy.' 'All right,' I responded, 'I will do my best, whatever is in my power I will do, you can be sure of that!' And I kept my word – all through the years these two kittens received greater care than any of their predecessors, resulting in two happy, physically healthy, felines.

It has always been my contention that if your work is your joy there is no problem, and I have had the satisfaction of gaining their love and affection, and their expressed appreciation for my efforts.

Some people consider it to be 'sissy', naive, and childish, to talk of love and affection but I do not see it that way; we never mind expressing dislike, hate, and resentment towards someone so, surely if we experience the reverse feeling, let us spread the sentiments. I appreciate those letters from readers of my previous books, when the writers tell me of their admiration for someone who is not afraid to express the love and affection with which their lives are surrounded. I have known the opposite, due in part to my own attitude, so I can now fully appreciate it is possible to experience 'heaven on earth', if you spend *some time* in giving a little thought to the needs of others. Who was it who said,

'Happiness is a by-product of some activity'? Was it Albert Einstein, I wonder! At any rate I have proved the truth of that statement, and perhaps I should now say, here endeth the lesson. It was not intended to be a sermon.

At the risk of being dubbed repetitive I have to comment a little on the period of several weeks until we finally left Fort Erie. The atmosphere had been what I can only call unfriendly, even hostile, following the publicity about the young man in England who had ended his own life.

One person who had been a neighbour and quite friendly suddenly 'cut' me completely when our paths would cross in the street, or if I had occasion to find myself in the store where she was employed. Possibly it was the one and only such experience of my life and I would not welcome another; the general antagonistic atmosphere.

This particular woman had a family and that was the furthest she could see – obviously thinking, 'Suppose it had been one of my children?' and that was the general opinion, just a one-sided judgement, and I mention the matter now because I want to put on record one of the Guv's opinions about mothers.

Lobsang Rampa believes that, in spite of their expressed love of their brood they are often guilty, whether deliberate or unintentional, or harming their children's interests. Often mothers are so biased that they are blind to what is best for their offspring. Too often possessiveness is the interpretation of love, and the Guv feels very strongly about it, often expressing the opinion that a mother *can* be a child's greatest enemy. Strong words but worth more than a thought. Look around and you will see the truth for yourself.

On the other hand I have always remembered one Fort Erie resident, also a parent, who showed real understanding towards us – an intelligent educated gentleman engaged in the business of electronics, particularly radio.

We met this person, periodically, in his small office which was adjoining his house outside the town, where he had a gigantic antenna attached to the roof. He had many similar interests to those of the Guv, so we often spent a few minutes chatting together. A busy man, his wife would contact him by an electric device, fitted to his car, while he might be on his way to head office, or distributor in Niagara Falls; that way he would save time as he might pick up supplies of goods the orders for which had been received by his office after he had left.

I have always had a very clear picture of this enlightened gentleman who operated classes for young people, on his spare evenings, teaching the mechanics of radio electronics.

The last time we had the opportunity of talking together was a chance meeting in the post office, just before we left the town when, on parting he said, 'Yes, I think you have suffered more than enough!'

It is better to 'have a thing out' rather than
to let it fester within.
It is not always a good thing to contain
annoyances or grievances; if you keep them
within yourself you will corrode your personality.

TWENTY

I believe we underestimate cats when we look upon them as
something which just sits around, preferably on the best
chair, always seeming to be asleep. Is there any other
domestic creature who is more alert to his surroundings,
who can seem to be sleeping (when he is not sleeping at all,
merely conserving his sight) when suddenly, at the merest
distraction, he is aroused, curious to investigate the cause
of the disturbance?

Cats are not so selfish as is thought; independent, yes,
but they are endowed with a great sense of responsibility
and, if treated fairly, they will reward us with extreme
devotion; they will try to protect their 'people' in face of
danger.

From the earliest days Miss Cleo and Miss Taddy were
inseparable, just as they had stayed together from the
moment they knew they were to be living together in the
same household, and one would not contemplate parting
them, even in separate rooms. If one of them happened to
be shut inside the storage closet she would not call to be
let out, but we would know because the other would just
sit outside the door, waiting.

A few weeks after they came to us Cleo seemed to have
something wrong with her right eye, which was watering,

and she couldn't seem to open it. Of course I was concerned and hurriedly telephoned Dr Reid who told me to bring Cleo along to his office immediately. That was the first time I realized how much these two little people cared about each other. I hurried off and left the Guv to deal with Taddy, who already looked alarmed at being left alone without her sister; fortunately we were soon home again, Dr Reid having put some drops in the eye, to find Taddy almost beside herself with anxiety. The Guv expressed great relief at our return.

Throughout their lives we always said that if one of them should get sick and have to go Home, we would probably have to let the other one go too, because we couldn't visualize one of them surviving alone. However we were not faced with the situation, fortunately, but if the blue one had been the survivor it might have been different; Taddy was very dependent upon Cleo, especially if her Ma was not available to provide companionship, and even so she could be quite strong willed to the point of obstinacy. Haven't you noticed it is the same with those humans who tend to lean on others – they are usually tough and full of obstinacy until they feel the need for reassurance? So, you see, cats *can* copy humans. Perhaps Taddy emulated Ma's behaviour! But not Cleo, who has always been affectionate – but independent.

Allowances always had to be made for Tadikins because she had a severe fright in the early period of her life, when she was no more than five months, and we were then staying in the Daniel's hotel in Prescott, Ontario, having left Fort Erie permanently about one month previously.

We were out in the passageway, leading to our rooms, when someone stampeded along, right past us, scaring Taddy half to death, resulting in an imbalance which pursued her for the remainder of her life. It would not have been so serious had she not been suffering from a physical disability, which affected her nervous system. Both kittens were beset with a hereditary condition of the bones, osteoporosis, which I did not know at the time; one day following the fright they were playing leapfrog together and suddenly Taddy collapsed, unable to walk, and I was quite concerned, rushing to the telephone for help.

I was told our new veterinarian Dr Wang, was unavailable, so I had to find another and he asked me to take Taddy along to his surgery where he would be waiting. Saturday noon, and when we arrived we found a most sympathetic listener to our problem. The young vet asked me to put my cat down on the floor so he might observe her; after watching her for a minute or so he expressed an opinion that it could be that her brain was damaged, thus affecting her walk and that he didn't hold out much hope for recovery. Even when listening to him, and hearing the worst, I couldn't help noticing his obvious concern which made it easier to accept the verdict. 'A real "humane" humanitarian,' I thought.

It was different when we reached home, however, for the Guv was full of concern and Cleo was beside herself with anxiety for her sister, and the anticipated loneliness for herself, for she knew all about the conversation with the veterinarian. All during that weekend there was an air of sadness and gloom radiating – to see baby cat making an effort to move herself. When she needed her sanitary tray she just dragged herself to it and it seemed miraculous how she dealt with the operation.

But there's always a bright side, especially if you are fortunate enough to have a Lobsang Rampa around, he who has said he believes life is too hard for so many people, defeating its aim to teach them anything.

Although the Guv had his own personal grief, he would

98

never do anything to make life's problems easier for himself, but he was terribly concerned for Cleo. He must have given the matter a lot of thought for, just as we were becoming somewhat reconciled to the thought of losing Taddy the Guv suddenly said. 'Cleo don't be worried for you will not lose your sister.' And again he spoke. 'Taddy, you *will* walk again. That is a promise.'

Thus happiness was restored, and we were to witness our little Blue-Grey autumn lady walking around once more – even running, in her own particular fashion.

> Had I but served my God as diligently as
> I served the King, he would not have
> given me over in my grey hairs.
>
> *Cardinal Wolsey –*
> *to Sir William Kingston*

FLYING HIGH

As I sit here in my room at five-thirty in the morning, facing downtown Calgary, away in the direction of Winnipeg and eastern Canada, everything is still and I see, less than one block distant, two construction cranes waiting to be activated.

One of the advantages of high-rise living is the opportunity for viewing life from on high, not quite so good as sitting in a helicopter where one might have a view from behind, in front and immediately below. The other day someone used the analogy in describing the Guv's amazing ability to see a person's life or events from the past, present and future.

I find there is a great deal to be learned from other people's remarks, especially from the letters of certain readers who are thoughtful enough to comment upon the Guv's books, and my own, in a constructive manner; the very few critical letters we receive come under the heading of 'hair splitting'.

At the risk of being accused of deviating from my own story I would like to pass on to those interested details of a little incident which occurred recently. One of our regular readers whose name is Marlene, wrote to tell us of a little blue budgie bird which had been brought to her, having been found near a golf course where she lives; it seemed to be suffering from exposure, she thought, so she placed it in a cage and went off to get some nourishment for the little creature. When Marlene returned she found the bird lying on the floor of the cage, apparently in some distress; she stayed with it for awhile then moved away to another room, where some household task required her attention.

'In a few seconds,' she wrote, 'I saw a ball of light enter the room where I was, much like you see around birds when they are flying.' She continued, 'Only this light was so much brighter and then I knew my little friend had gone to the place where all bird people go.' Further, 'That's the first time I ever saw a spirit on its way Home.'

I hope someone will appreciate that little incident; because of her heightened vibrations through her consideration for the sick bird she had been able to 'tune in', and she had felt a surge of gratitude from its spirit as it departed.

Judging by our correspondence there seems to be a wave of good feelings towards nature people and, since we are on the subject of birds, I might mention another delightful request which came to the Guv. Someone wrote, 'If you care to send me any advice on how to give my bird people a more even break it would be greatly appreciated by us all. They are so enduring and touching.' And she included a sketch of a somewhat bedraggled baby sparrow who had been too active and fallen from the nest, and had been rescued by our correspondent. The caption read, 'This is sort of how a new boarder looked.'

The lady, who has at least two birds of her own, welcomed the little sparrow. 'Now he has a new home,' she says, 'and he is quite sweet.'

She ended her letter by telling us she looks forward with pleasure to reading about the autumn lady.

This section seems to be all about flying, which reminds

me that Miss Taddy and Miss Cleo spent much time in the air, flying high in a Lear jet once or twice when we undertook a long journey from Montreal to Vancouver and, previously, between Saint John, New Brunswick, to Montreal.

Sometimes one of our more critical readers will tell us our books are repetitive, while others, more tolerant, will not mind repetition; indeed they remark that it is helpful and welcome our repeats. However, in deference to the former I will try to present the few incidents, which may already have been documented in my previous books, in a slightly different manner; since the story is about Tadalinka a little repetition seems unavoidable.

Miss Cleo and her Ma, as we sit here at the typewriter, Cleo tuned in and helping retrace the interesting life we have had, both realize that we have plenty of happy memories to sustain us, and we can now take life more quietly; not have to be dashing around the country.

Just last year, when we vaguely discussed another move, Cleo and Taddy were most unhappy. 'No more moves for us,' they told the Guv. 'We've had enough, more than, and we would rather go Home.' So the family stayed here and, except for Taddy, here we remain. As for Taddy 'the owl called her name' so she had to go. There is, in the lore of the American Indian, a belief that when your time comes to depart, if the owl has called your name you have no choice but to go.

The Guv has just told me that Cleo often finds amusement in remembering an incident which occurred while we were living in New Brunswick. She had seemed to have a fever, was refusing food and appeared generally lethargic, so we arranged to visit the local veterinarian. While travelling in a taxi to his office in Rothesay we were almost involved in an accident, a car cutting right in front of us, and I felt that literally, I 'jumped out of myself in fright'. It was only providential protection, what we call 'lucky stars', which saved us, I am sure!

'So what's so funny about that?' you say. That was not the cause of Miss Cleo's mirth – rather it was when the vet visited her at home after she had been sick for a few days, with a slightly elevated temperature. After examining the thermometer intently for a few seconds, the vet exclaimed, 'It must be pneumonia. Look at this, it's about one hundred and five.' That was before Celsius – I hope. She didn't look all that sick to me – and then I remembered – she was sitting on a rubber hot water bottle.

Fortunately the vet from the Netherlands possessed a sense of humour so we all laughed, including Cleo. Throughout the years, since she was little more than a baby the incident has never ceased to amuse he dignified Cleopatra.

Words are the dress of thoughts
which should no more be presented in rags,
tatters, and dirt, than your person should.

Earl of Chesterfield

TWENTY-ONE

Sunday morning, late in May, and at last we have signs that
summer will soon be here; this is the day one sets aside as
special to the Family. We are fortunate in having a nice,
secluded balcony leading off the living room and that is
where Miss Taddy loved to be whenever possible. If ever
a cat wore a smile of satisfaction it could be seen in Taddy's
expression, as she settled herself on the long garden chair,
or rolled the big, plump, fur-covered package which was
Tadikins, over and over on the green 'indoor outdoor' carpet which graces our balcony.

I do not know whether the expression 'indoor outdoor' is
used outside North America, but it seemed strange to me
when I first heard it in New Brunswick – the manager was
having this marvellous carpet installed at the entrance of
our building, and inside the lobby. 'Oh yes,' he explained.
'This is something new. It is not harmed by water and in
winter, especially, we use it because here we have quite a
number of older people who might have trouble on the slip-
pery floors.'

I could see his point since I had slipped on the icy entrance
more than once, and this floor covering did away with the
polished smoothness, snow and ice being simply absorbed.

So Taddy enjoyed the morning, and noontime sun; being
extremely voluble she talked a great deal to her Ma. Al-

though she departed in the fall of last year it is now that I think of her more than ever – as I put out the cushions on the redwood garden chairs I sense her presence, and I picture her with a wide smile on her face.

About two years ago I decided to have a big umbrella outside, to shelter us from the hot summer sun, and it caused much speculation – from a feline angle. Since I had no sand to put in the container to hold the umbrella down, I had it filled with water, and the stem was placed through a hole in a wooden table, which was also used for meals.

It was amusing to see the interest shown by Cleo and Taddy while watching all this being assembled by Keith, who wanted to do it before embarking on the same programme himself.

When it was all over I asked the Guv what Cleo and Taddy thought about it since he never minds translating from 'Cat'. 'Oh,' he informed me, with a smile, 'they consider you have been installing a parachute.' I liked that! Most cat-people love the sun and I believe Taddy had a particular reason for what was almost an obsession with her, and this might be a suitable moment to relate a little of the autumn lady's previous history:

During quiet moments, which are quite frequent in our home, the Guv would often converse with Taddy, telepathically, and they had many interesting discussions.

You see Taddy was lethargic in the physical sense, always conserving her energy, except when she heard the music of a can opener or when she sensed that I was slicing a piece of raw meat for her, but mentally she was extremely alert, and she was known as the telephone girl who helped the Guv. Some people may consider this far fetched, but others will understand and, after all, it is the latter who are interested in furthering their relationship with their cat companions. When you know TRUTH you do not need fiction.

People make a mistake if they insist on disturbing a cat when it appears to be sleeping – the lazy wretch, they think, and that is one reason why they often prefer to be in a home without children, especially untrained ones. Cats spend at least half their time sailing around in a state which, for want of a better term, one might call astral travelling; I have heard the Guv tell how they cast around when they are feeling sociable, looking for another cat with whom to hold a conversation, especially if they have an interesting piece of information. Oh yes, cats have a sense of humour and they tell jokes to each other.

Well, during these conversations between the Guv and Fat Taddy they talked about her life before she came to us, how she had twice tried to be with us and how she was determined to make another effort, even if it meant getting herself born into a family of seal point Siamese.

'Yes,' she had said to the Guv, 'I knew all about you, well not *all* but enough to make the effort worthwhile, because I was tired of living life after life in the wilds.' She said she wanted to be a domestic cat for a change.

Later the Guv related much of Taddy's history and, of course, I was an avid listener when he told me that our autumn lady had been a tree cat, a big creature such as a puma wild cat, and that she had lived in the rain forests of South America, specifically Brazil where, according to the information she gave, and verified by the Guv, she had spent hours upon hours just idly dreaming her life away – not one life but many.

Interestingly, many times she had developed a soreness – the result of which had caused her life to end in an unhappy manner, when the sore became infected. Taddy told of how the condition had persisted for a number of incarnations, and the Guv agreed with her when she said the soreness started because she sat too long on a tree where a small 'knot' irritated her skin, which eventually broke, became infected, which condition brought about her death, not once but through many lives.

So the time must have arrived when she was allowed to change her course, and see what she would make of different circumstances, with its new opportunities.

One might dramatize the situation but since it is the truth, why bother? Why gild the lily?

One cannot but admire someone who shows such single minded ambition, and in Taddy's case the effort paid off.

Lauren Bacall wrote in her recently published autobiography that she was *besotted* with her small son; I know how she felt, for I adored my autumn lady. Taddy herself would be the first to admit that *she* was not quite normal in her reactions, for she openly discussed it with the Guv. She said it was all right, for then no one would expect too much of her.

Perhaps it was because of this that she meant so much to me. We all like to feel someone is dependent upon us – it makes us feel worthwhile – and that is how it was with Tadalinka. Her dependence was utter and complete – shared with the lovely Cleo who showed her more tolerance than anyone might expect. When Taddy felt motherly she would wash and nibble Cleo's ears to distraction. So much so that we thought Cleo's 'dog-eared' appearance indicated she was in need of a vitamin supplement.

Because of Taddy I understood how a mother feels towards her retarded child – the complete trust of the child who at times seems almost angelic in its innocence. It provides a wonderful outlet for the protective instinct with which most of us are endowed.

Far away there in the sunshine
are my highest aspirations.
I may not reach them, but I can look up
and see their beauty, believe in them,
and try to follow where they lead.

Louisa May Alcott

TWENTY-TWO

What an interesting situation! Here was I, Ma to these cat-persons whose background and history had been so different from each other. On the one hand there was the mountain lion, she of the wild, who had never before known domes-ticity; whose purr could be loud and sonorous; whose growl when displeased was enough to intimidate the bravest vet, and her spitting hiss caused the onlooker to gape, amazed at her ferocity. And yet when resting on her special chair, or curled up on the arm of her Ma, she was the gentlest creature, full of love and affection. That was our Fat Taddy Cat – learning how to become civilized, away from the jungle.

Then the contrast, in the form of Miss Cleopatra, who had lived many lives among the human race, often with an aristocratic family; whose previous life had ended prematurely, through cruelty, and who had carried over to the present life her fear of men. She had planned to be difficult, to 'get her own back' for the way she had been mistreated by humanity. At first she would move away from the Guv and, when he had ascertained the reason for her problem, he took her aside and talked to her, after which time her attitude changed; she became the Guv's cat, while Taddy gravitated towards her Ma. The Guv often reminds me that this creature, all six pounds of her, is one of the most evolved entities, either animal or human, who has ever crossed our path; that she had never been known to express an unkind thought.

Through the years those two cat-persons have complemented each other, absolutely; since they were so different from each other there never was any cause for jealousy, or resentment, qualities not uncommon in the Siamese species. Cleo educated Taddy all about sophistication, about the lives of the upper echelon of society, how to behave – in short Cleo taught much about good manners. Taddy, on the other hand regaled Cleo with stories of the jungle, how when you are really BIG, humans, and small creatures, are afraid of you, so you can get what you want.

As these two persons gradually established themselves in the household they seemed to arrive at an agreement, they had a pact whereby each would agree not to encroach upon the other's territory.

Although Miss Taddy had enjoyed sitting on the Guv's bed when she was a kitten, Cleo gradually assumed the role of caring for him, and Taddy was allowed to sit by the door as observer. Sometimes she would arrange herself in such a position so that we could see, from the depths of the room, only half her face, only one eye, and it was really quite amusing to watch.

Taddy was just as firm regarding her territory for if she might be sitting side by side with me, purring contentedly, and Cleo came towards us, Taddy would cease her purr; bristling up she would scold Cleo soundly, and my little Cleo, who also needed her Ma, would have to move away. How I would have enjoyed it had we all be able to sit down together but, no, the strong willed Taddy would have none of it. It was the same when we retired for the night, Taddy was waiting to rest on my arm long before I was ready for her. We settled down and a few minutes later Cleo would arrive; having surveyed the territory she might make her way under the covers when immediately, Taddy would leave my arm and pounce on the covers just where Cleo had settled. A wild cat, always hunting!

I am going to relate a true story concerning Taddy, especially for those who believe that cats are thinking entities which means those people who have read my other books and believed in them. I would not wish it to be thought I was in the same state as poor Louis Wain, who became so involved with cats, being able to communicate with them, and executing detailed drawings of them, that his mind became deranged, and he ended his days in an institution.

The story is true, because she told it to the Guv – during the whole of her life Taddy would intimate to the Guv that she was expecting a package to be delivered to her. 'What is in it?' I would ask, and the reply would be, 'Never mind what is in it. It is from Brazil.' So Taddy was mixed up about her incarnations, but it was not surprising since her life there had ended prematurely.

Periodically, we would be reminded, 'I am still waiting for it!' It was not until some weeks after she had left the earth that Miss Cleo received a telepathic message, 'I don't think it will ever come. I guess my Mother never sent it.' If you cannot accept that story well, you can read it as a pretty fairy tale. All the same it is very real!

Referring to incarnations I would recommend the book, *Audrey Rose* by Frank deFelitta. It was sent to us by one of our publishers and I never would have *bought* such a title, which would have been my loss. The book and the film have been a great success, and it was while I was read-

ing the story that I decided to document the lives of Tadalinka, which I felt sure would be of interest to those readers
who believe in the continuing cycle of death and rebirth.

'Twould ring the bells of Heaven
The wildest peal for years,
If Parson lost his senses
And people came to theirs,
And he and they together
Knelt down with angry prayers
For tame and shabby tigers,
And dancing dogs and bears,
And wretched, blind pit ponies,
And little hunted hares.

Ralph Hodgson

TWENTY-THREE

After moving around, first in Ontario, then to other provinces, namely, New Brunswick, Quebec and British
Columbia, we finally found a resting place with the wild
rose of Alberta, which has been our home for almost six
years. I would never have expected our travels would take
us to Stampede City, which just goes to show you never
know what the future has in store.

For me, personally, this was a good move; the high alti-
tude seems to keep me mentally alert and it is here in Calgary that I have been able to fulfil a life-long ambition to
do some writing. Although one never can be sure of anything, at this moment it would seem that the remainder of
my days will be spent here, where Cleo, Taddy, and I have
spent some of our happiest moments.

A big city with a population totalling more than half a
million, we still have a somewhat parochial outlook, possibly due to the fact that the city has grown too quickly,

accepting even now about two thousand immigrants from other provinces, each month.

One of the blots on our reputation is the way we treated our leading kidney transplant surgeon, Dr Abouna, as though he were a criminal, except that a criminal would have received more consideration. That affair was enough to make one feel ashamed. Then a Catholic school superintendent was dismissed for no apparent reason; the board of governors have never seen fit to provide an explanation. These two cases are still receiving much publicity, though Dr Abouna is far away, continuing his work with great success.

Ah, well, we are a young country, that is our excuse, but we will grow up, given time.

Life went on smoothly enough, until late last summer, when we noticed a small lump on Taddy's 'undercarriage'; it may have been present for some days before it was noticed. As soon as possible we notified Dr Randall, who came along to see her, and he said we would have to observe the swelling to see whether it would disappear, or the reverse. The situation entailed several visits, each time Dr Randall measured to see if it had become bigger, and one day I said I thought it was smaller but he shook his head in sympathy at my optimism.

It was suggested the lump should be removed, when we might hope for a few months respite before Taddy would succumb, so I went along to tell the Guv. We decided to put aside our own feelings which meant trying to keep her with us, and consider Taddy who would suffer through an operation – so it would be better to let things take their natural course for whatever length of time she would be spared to us, which proved to be short.

One Sunday, in the early autumn, Taddy's condition worsened, and we knew she would not be with us much longer. The Guv came out to the living room, as I told him I was concerned about her. He spoke to Taddy, looked at her lingeringly, and then he uttered the words which I dreaded hearing, 'I think it's time to say goodbye,' and he went back to his room.

I had been enquiring the previous week whether Dr Randall would be on duty that holiday weekend, and he assured me he would be so I called him, when he asked me to place her in her large, comfortable travelling basket, and he would meet us at his office that Sunday afternoon; he considered it better than coming to us, which would have been more distressing for her and for all of us.

She loved the journey with her Ma, though she must have felt very unwell, since the sore was suppurating, and the Guv wanted me to hurry while she didn't seem to be having actual pain.

Dr Randall greeted us with understanding, then he took charge of the situation, preparing Taddy for her journey to Cat land, giving her a mild injection, then because she was big, another. It was all so smooth, our Taddy just drifting away to be met with all the others in what we know as the Cat's Heaven. After chatting awhile I came out to the taxi, with a heavy heart.

When I arrived home all was quiet and the Guv told me Taddy had not felt any pain, merely a dreamy, drifting feeling and I could not believe it for her expression had shown she was going to a place where she was wanted, and where she would be welcomed with love. Had I understood 'cat language' I might have heard her remark, with Thomas Edison, in his final moments, 'Isn't it beautiful over there.'

Because our association with his family extends rather beyond the professional, Dr Randall asked me if I would like Taddy's last resting place to be in his own garden, to which suggestion I was pleased to agree. So, during the weekend the doctor's son, Jamie, undertook the preparations, proud to do something for a friend; so that is where our Taddy's physical frame rests. We were grateful to Jamie, who is thirteen, and believes he is going to be a vet himself, unless he chooses forestry, another of his interests. Veterinary work entails much study and high grades, he says!

When it was all over the Guv told me, 'You were just in time – much longer and she would have suffered, from peritonitis.' So we sighed, and resumed our normal routine while there has always been a sense of loss, but Taddy still comes around, in another form, and I always have to leave the usual night-light on for her. She says she stumbles when it is too dark.

I believe that her life was a success, and that when we meet again, we will all be together for a long time, working together as we did down here! Taddy will be plagued no longer with the sores of several lifetimes and she will always be grateful to Lobsang Rampa, 'Guv of all the cats' who, in showing his respect for our autumn lady, discontinued using the logo which had graced his paper heading for some years.

It occurred to me that actions speak very much louder than words; if your feelings are deep you do not necessarily talk about your grief – you act. The Guv's sensitivity is so much greater than my own, therefore he feels things more keenly, be it joy or sadness!

Isn't it beautiful over there.

Words attributed to Thomas Edison
towards the end of his life.
He seemed to be looking at something beyond.

CANADA CUSTOMS

Gilberto, our Spanish speaking friend from Central America, has always been a great fan of our Siamese people, and each time he writes to me he never fails to make reference to Cleo and Taddy; Gilberto shows his friendship in many ways.

One day I received a notice from the Federal Customs Department in this city, intimating they had a parcel awaiting collection, and the customer's card, describing the contents, merely stated 'porcelain figure'. Away I went to customs and I was greeted by an official who indicated he needed an invoice, or a statement, showing the value of the goods. I was not able to provide anything – but when I was shown the contents I asked if I might take the parcel then and there. 'Oh, no! You can't do that before you first contact the sender to find out the value! You must write to the person who sent the gift, meanwhile the parcel will stay here.' 'But it will be perhaps three weeks or four until I receive an answer,' I told the official. 'Anyhow, it is not easy to ask someone the value of their gift,' I continued.

After giving the matter some thought the manager was called, so together they had a discussion, while I was eager to get my hands on that figure a foot high of a young girl, with long brown hair, sitting on a high-backed chair holding a blue point Siamese on her lap, encircled within her arms, and a sealpoint sat beside her on the base. 'We–ell,' said the manager, 'if you are prepared to accept our appraisal and come again tomorrow you may have it.' So what could I do but accept, hoping the charges would not be excessive.

Sometimes it is necessary to refuse an unsolicited gift, especially if one has not been notified by the sender; however this parcel was from Gilberto *and I had seen the contents*, so the next day found me there again at the Customs office, eager to know if the matter of charges had been settled.

'Oh, there you are,' said the official, when he saw me. 'I will get your parcel.'

When he returned I asked him how much there was to pay.

'Forty dollars, please,' he told me, so I took the papers to the cashier, paid the duty and federal taxes, returned the receipts to the official, took my parcel and hurried home.

This figure is one of my most treasured possessions, Cleo and Taddy immortalized in ceramic gives me great satisfaction, providing an atmosphere of peace and contentment.

Tiger, Tiger, burning bright
In the forests of the night,
What immortal hand or eye
Could frame thy fearful symmetry?

William Blake

TWENTY-FOUR

If we could understand cat language, cat telepathy or whatever, we would enter a new exciting world, but at the same time we need to have our metaphorical feet placed firmly on the ground, thus hoping to retain our sanity and matter-of-factness. Why do I mention this? Well the Guv has explained to me how cats make pictures which to another cat are easily decipherable but to any human who *has* the ability to see the pictures, it is necessary to cultivate a slightly different way of reasoning before being able to translate.

We might all be sitting in the Guv's room when suddenly he exhorts us to be quiet while he receives a 'cat message' and then he will smile, telling us about the pictures formed and how at first he couldn't 'get it'.

One evening, in particular, Taddy was having a telepathic conversation with another cat-person and they were talking about 'riding the range' – it seemed that neither of them had a clear picture so the Guv had to decipher their meaning after seeing a picture of a cooking stove – a range! You need to be quick-witted to understand cat language; the Guv is and *does*.

Before coming to the end of *Autumn Lady* I have promised three cat-people to include them here, because they have provided interest and one of them was the means whereby I made a new and interesting association with his so-called mistress, who is really his slave.

First I must tell you about Smooch, whom I have known the longest, and who lives with an Austrian family about two blocks nearer the river, that is, two blocks from the building where I live.

Smooch's 'slave' is Loni who comes here every week to help me clear out the debris and dust which accumulates all too frequently in this apartment. We have known Loni for a period of nearly four years and she can always be relied upon to help out in an emergency. She has nursing experience, too.

Well, late one afternoon the telephone bell rang and I hurried to find out who was there, since we do not have many calls.

'Mrs Rampa, can you help me,' a concerned voice rang out. 'It is Loni, and I wonder if you can lend me a cat basket.'

'What happened?' I asked, noting the air of concern. After a pause, 'It's Smooch, I think he has a broken leg, he is sitting under a chair and we can't go near him.'

'What makes you think his leg is broken?' I asked. 'Well, he came into the house dragging one leg,' she said. Apparently he was in considerable pain and the family didn't know what to do.

Loni's son, Ralph, came to borrow a travelling basket but he said he didn't think he would be able to coax Smooch into it. I thought about it, then decided to consult Dr Randall whose surgery hours would be ending in a few minutes, at six o'clock.

It's always useful to have a good relationship with your veterinarian and this was one time when I appreciated it, because Dr Randall said he would go to see the cat after

119

he had completed another house call, since no one could approach Smooch and the office would be closed anyway.

Later that evening I heard that Smooch had become an unwilling guest of the Westside Pet Hospital, and that his stay would last a few days. The 'fracture' was not serious, but the rather badly lacerated leg needed instant attention, and he was given an antibiotic.

We understand Smooch does not venture out so much these days, not being so young he is not anxious to get involved in any more fights, which might mean another stay in the hospital.

Cat number two has a different story; whenever we think of her we feel like 'smiling loudly' though her mistress-slave probably would not see it that way at all.

Enter Loni again. Telephone rings. I rush to answer. 'What shall I do with this cat who has come to my door?' 'What do you mean?' I ask. 'Which cat?'

'Well, I heard crying outside in the garden and on going to the back door I saw this little cat; I think it is a Siamese and I really don't know what to do with it.' So Loni had a problem which she hoped I could solve.

Another call to our special cat doctor who said we should take her to the office; he was sure he could find a home worthy of a Siamese, unless her owner traced and claimed her within about a week, the time he would have to keep her, before allowing her to go to another home. She was not a stray, he said, because she was in very good condition; she wore a collar, but without a name on it.

If anyone had asked me about the creature I would have told them, 'Well she knew, or thought she knew, of a vacancy in the Rampa household; believing the Rampa cat people lead the good life (which they do), she probably thought, "Perhaps I could fill the gap left vacant by Fat Cat Taddy. I understand Miss Cleo is a very good companion."

As I have stated, cats have a greater intelligence than they are credited with and Miss Siamese would know Loni was associated with us, so she had nothing to lose. She couldn't have come straight to us because a cat is not expected to gain access to an apartment building, operate an elevator, and get transported to a certain floor. How would she activate the elevator motor – the button was too high! So she did the next best thing – called upon Loni.

Habits are first cobwebs, then cables.

Spanish proverb

TWENTY-FIVE

Here enters our friend Gertrud who I am sure will not mind being brought into the story because I mentioned I would do so and since she did not object I guess it is okay with her.

We were chatting together one day when it occurred to me to ask Gertrud how she would like to have a cat in her household.

'You never can tell,' she answered, 'but what have you in mind?' So I explained about the Siamese which was being boarded at the Westside Hospital, and to my slight surprise Gertrud appeared interested. 'The only thing which concerns me,' she went on, 'is my two dogs, whether the cat will accept them, and they her!' One of her dogs, being blind, might have a problem in adjusting.

I assured her that dogs usually have no trouble with Siamese and Siamese in turn do not seem to mind sharing a home with a dog.

We lost no time in contacting the Pet Hospital, letting Dr Randall know we had found a suitable human who would like to provide a home for the little cat person. Within a few days Gertrud's responsibilities had begun – and Shara's new life started. Many preparations had been made and the cat was allotted a special room in the house; she was allowed to share Gertrud's study.

All went well for some days after Shara's arrival, except when she was introduced to the doggies, when she aired her opinion by way of a growl and a hiss. This happened each time the three came together, so Shara had to be kept separate from the dogs, a situation which she did not enjoy, and which she planned to change!

When things seemed to be somewhat settled, and after Gertrud found herself minus her pet bird, after the cage had inadvertently been left open, we had a call from her; she seemed to be in some distress.

'My cat has gone,' she said and I asked her what had happened. 'Well this is my day off and I was doing a little housework; I was going into the garden to shake out some rugs. As I opened the door Shara suddenly appeared, speeding like a streak of lightning and, before I could stop her, she was over my moderately high wire fence, and away she went.'

Gertrud had spent all morning trying to find her, calling and waiting, but there was no sign of Shara. Obviously she wanted her freedom and one wonders whether she was a flower child, a hippie cat. Since Gertrud was so upset the Guv did a bit of investigating by his own particular method, and he was able to assure her that Shara had been adopted by another family, when she had tried her luck in another direction where there were no canine, or feline competition. A determined young lady cat! The Guv ascertained the Shara cat had been under a death sentence from an apartment owner who said, 'No cats' – so her previous family had abandoned her.

Mr Boots, or Bootsie is cat-person number three and he is the youngest, still not having reached his first birthday but already he has experienced a number of changes in his young life.

This little person was found last year in a Calgary lumber yard, along with his mother, sisters and brothers. A family of strays, the cat mother was about to depart this life, as were a few of her babies, all of whom were suffering from

123

starvation through malnutrition; the mother herself, being underfed, could not possibly provide sustenance for her kittens.

A friendly human came along and found one little creature still living, so Boots finally found his way to his human Mother, Lee, a young career woman housewife, who has been able to provide all the love and nutrition necessary for his welfare.

I have met Bootsie a few times but I do not know whether our paths will cross again for, just this week, Lee finds her government position will entail a transfer away from this province. Since I do not expect to visit Eastern Canada in the future it is unlikely I will have the pleasure of watching the progress of beautiful Mr Boots, who has already made the journey where he will stay with friends while mistress Lee organizes her own house move.

My story brings us right up to the past week, a week of many changes which just goes to remind us how we should make the most of the present which even now is moving forward towards the future, with further change.

Recently the Shah of Iran was interviewed and he was quoted as saying that everything which had happened was God's will, the will of Allah. 'Do you consider it was God's will that caused you to lose your position as head of your country?' the interviewer asked. 'Yes,' said the Shah, 'to show that nothing remains the same!'

I am going to end this book with a few verses from an unknown author, which might well be titled 'Don't Wait,' and which could easily have been composed by that Fat Cat Taddy, the autumn lady, whose concepts it embraces. Except, whoever heard of a composing cat!

When I quit this mortal shore,
And mosey around this earth no more,
Don't weep, don't sigh, don't sob –
I may have struck a better job.

Don't go and buy a large bouquet
For which you'll find it hard to pay;
Don't mope around and feel all blue –
I may be better off than you.

Don't tell folks I was a saint,
Or any old thing that I ain't;
IF YOU HAVE JAM LIKE THAT TO SPREAD
Please hand it out before I'm dead.

If you have roses, bless your soul,
Just pin one in my buttonhole
While I'm alive and well today –
Don't wait until I'm gone away.

Author unknown

From Seasons of Inspiration

If you wish to write to the Author, please address your
letters to BM/RAAB, Monomark House, London W.C.1.

PUSSYWILLOW by MAMA SAN RA-AB RAMPA

You will be amused, delighted and entranced by Mama San's account of life with her famous husband and their beloved Siamese cats. Miss Ku'ei, Fifi, Sindhi the Baby Cat, Cleo and Taddy will make their engaging feline way into your affections: Cat lovers everywhere will enjoy the entertaining descriptions of these fascinating cat-people and their pranks.

Mama San, like her husband, is both wise and compassionate, and her gentle philosophy of life will afford comfort and inspiration to the countless followers of T. Lobsang Rampa.

0 552 10261 X   50p

I BELIEVE by T. LOBSANG RAMPA

'This book will tell of life before birth, Life on Earth, and the passing from Earth and return to Life Beyond . . .'

This is Lobsang Rampa's seventeenth book. In previous books he has written about his early life, his training at the Lamasery and his battles against the forces of evil in the world. Now, in response to overwhelming requests from his devoted followers all over the world, he has set down his beliefs about life after death – the testimony of a remarkable teacher that will bring comfort to his countless readers and shed the light of inspiration on this the greatest of human mysteries.

0 552 10416 7   75p

A SELECTED LIST OF PSYCHIC, MYSTIC AND OCCULT BOOKS THAT APPEAR IN CORGI

ORDER FORM

All these books are available at your bookshop or newsagent, or can be ordered direct from the publisher. Just tick the titles you want and fill in the form below.

CORGI BOOKS, Cash Sales Department, P.O. Box 11, Falmouth, Cornwall.

Please send cheque or postal order, no currency.

U.K. send 25p for first book plus 10p per copy for each additional book ordered to a maximum charge of £1.05 to cover the cost of postage and packing.

B.F.P.O. and Eire allow 25p for first book plus 10p per copy for the next eight books, thereafter 5p per book.

Overseas Customers. Please allow 40p for the first book and 12p per copy for each additional book.

NAME (block letters) ....

ADDRESS ....

....

While every effort is made to keep prices low, it is sometimes necessary to increase prices at short notice. Corgi books reserve the right to show new retail prices on covers which may differ from those previously advertised in the text or elsewhere.